Past-Forward

Past-Forward

A three-decade and three-thousand-mile journey home

-Maureen K. Wlodarczyk

Outskirts Press, Inc.
Denver, Colorado

Outskirts Press, Inc.
http://www.outskirtspress.com

ISBN: 978-1-4327-5225-5

Outskirts Press and the "OP" logo are trademarks belonging to Outskirts Press, Inc.

PRINTED IN THE UNITED STATES OF AMERICA

*For Arlene, Kate, Mamie and
all the mothers of our clan*

*When this you see, pray think of these
and keep them in your mind*

Contents

Introduction i

A Promise Kept 1

So Close But So Far Away 5

Traveling the Technological Highway 13

Ashes to Ashes, Time Stands Still 19

In the Beginning 25

Sligo Is No More 41

Out of Ireland 49

Farewell, farewell and what is more,
Receive my blessing from this shore 55

None but the Frugal, Industrious, and Temperate 59

Community and Catholicism 67

The Jersey Blues 73

Another Bridget "Such-a-One" Journeys to America 85

Not Lost, Just Gone Before 93

On the Cobblestone Streets of Jersey City............................. 101

Let All the World Say What They Will,
Speak of Me as You Find.. 109

And Yet to Every Bad, There is a Worse................................. 121

The White Plague 125

A Tale of Two Sisters... 129
Wife and Mother...and Daughter........................ 137
Marking Time... 143
Descendants of Owen Flannelly........................ 147
Bibliography 151

Introduction

I am a DNA dead-end. The journey of a genetic signature that originated tens of thousands of years ago and wound its way through the ages, the eras, the centuries, and generations of my maternal ancestors to fuse into my being at the moment of my own conception ends with me. Truthfully, absent recent genetic research and the general publication of resulting findings and my lifelong preoccupation with my "roots," I would not even have known I was the last stop on an incredible journey of survival and rebirth. In the context of the history or evolution of what we know as "the human race," my "situation" is not a rare occurrence or significant event...except to me.

Maternal DNA, called mitochondrial DNA or MtDNA, is passed by mothers to all their children, male or female, but only daughters pass it on to the next generation. That means that the MtDNA passed on by mother to daughter for thousands of years remains essentially the very same MtDNA. Mine is the same as that of my maternal great-great-grandmother, Delia Hough Flannelly, born in Ireland in the mid-nineteenth century, and it is the same as that of *her* maternal great-great-grandmother. The river of MtDNA that originated in some ancient time tens of thousands of years ago flowed forth down the generations, thrusting off tributaries that spawned streams, those streams giving birth to delicate rivulets, each carrying the seeds of MtDNA to succeeding generations. Whenever a woman does not give birth to a daughter, she becomes a DNA dam, a DNA dead-end…like me. The universe is full of twinkling MtDNA stars and every day some of them burn out.

For thirty-five years, I have felt a persistent need to discover and piece together my ethnic ancestry and origins. My forays in search of the stories of those who came before me were sporadic, punctuated as time, family obligations, and finances allowed. But, I never "stopped," never lost interest and never surrendered no matter how many times I hit the proverbial wall. It's been more of a calling and a form of "completing" myself rather than a goal or objective or even a choice. For those of you bitten by the same bug, no explanation is required. For the many others who don't "get it," I understand…really. I sometimes explain it using an analogy and image that has lived in my mind for lo these many years and which has been made "real" by the passage of time and the attendant loss of older family members and generations. Ancestral family lines are like a chain woven of many, many links. When we are born we are shiny new links added in extension of that chain. There are many older (and elder) relatives whose links have become weathered but who nonetheless provide a sturdy tether to those from whom and whence we came and so to the fabric of who we are. Over the intervening years, the most worn and aged of these chain links will fall away and our own links begin to weather as well. Ultimately, we feel the loss of the links behind us and recognize that we are replacing those who have been lost, becoming the "old" links. Said another way, our relatives and our family history give us "connectivity," "continuity," and "context." Ask an adoptee raised by loving adoptive parents who yet undertakes a search for their birth parent. Connectivity, continuity, context…

My three-decade search for my Irish family roots has been an amazing, frustrating, joyful, sad, challenging, serendipitous, surprising, and enriching set of experiences and discoveries. Imagine tackling the scavenger hunt of a lifetime with the zeal of a life or death mission. Each hunted bit or piece the potential promise of a clue or revelation or intuitive whisper of direction. These singular fragments, viewed in retrospect, meshed together into a fantastic crazy quilt of people and places stitched together to reveal a poignant story of the past. I have found relations in the US and in the "old country" and they have become part of my extended family and my life. I have cried with joy when the mysteries of the distant past were finally revealed and I have wept bitter tears knowing the suffering, persecution, and deprivation that forced my Irish ancestors to leave the land and family they loved. The eighteenth-century German writer Jean Paul Richter wrote: "Memories are the only paradise from which we can never be expelled" but there is another side to that coin: memories can also be a prison that we must escape. Most family stories, including mine, are threaded with both.

Back in the days of black-and-white TV, when I was in elementary school, I decided I would be an archaeologist when I grew up. I can't recall what precipitated or influenced that decision but the decision itself is crystal clear in my memory. It was probably the first tangible manifestation of my affinity for things historical and ancient. I also liked to sketch, which would have come in handy on those digs in Egypt I was imagining and planning. I had a cherished Jon Gnagy "Learn to Draw" set that I used to hone my artistic skills. I can still smell the scent of those "professional" gum erasers! Somehow, in the ensuing years and crosswinds of puberty, those career plans derailed and suddenly, inspired by my Barbie, I was sketching clothes and fancying myself a future fashion designer.

Even so, the draw of the past was still with me and was fueling a more personal curiosity. Growing up, my grandmothers, one of Irish descent and the other born in Italy, were very important to me. Their love was a special treasure and I enjoyed spending time with them and hearing stories about the past. I admired and looked up to them for their strength in dealing with the ups and downs of their lives, one having had a very difficult childhood and the other having emigrated from a place she loved and still missed. In my eyes, they were unique, strong, and even heroic, and just, in a word, *special*. Perhaps because of that, I have always worn my ethnicity with great pride, believing that we should never forget from whom and whence we came. Decades before DNA testing and the amazing things it can tell us about our origins, I felt compelled to keep faith with my ancestral past by discovering it, documenting it, and perpetuating it by sharing it with my children and other family members.

In my early twenties, I sat down with each of my grandmothers and asked them to tell me about their childhood and share any family stories from the "olden days." In turn, I put pen to paper and wrote down what each of them told me in a circa-1970 spiral notebook whose cover depicted what would now be described as a "hippie" couple romping through the grass with four "flower power" motif balloons, each emblazoned with the word *Love*. Thirty-plus years later, I still have that treasured dog-eared relic and I have read and re-read the entries dozens and dozens of times…just in case I missed something. The truth is that what I missed was the opportunity to ask more and better questions in follow-up to those original notes. So many years later and so much more experienced, I can think of a hundred questions I could have and should have asked each of them. In giving pointers to others who are setting off to "find themselves," I now make it a point to emphasize the importance of seeking out the oldest living family members, including extended family and even estranged family if you can get their cooperation. Besides being rich sources of information about the past in general, there is the real possibility that they will provide a specific fragment that, although seemingly insignificant on its own, turns out to be a key piece in solving that jigsaw puzzle of yours.

Since my father and my Italian grandparents were born in their ancestral village in Italy, there was no doubt where that part of my heritage was rooted. My grandmother provided the names of her parents and her grandparents and the names of my grandfather's parents, all having come from the same village, Montorio Nei Frentani, Campobasso, in Molise.

Not so for my Irish-descended grandmother, Kate. Her childhood had been a short and turbulent one. Over multiple conversations, she told me about her mother's early death of "consumption" (aka tuberculosis), that her father turned his motherless children over to the care of various relatives, subsequently joined the Army, and played no further role in their lives. She believed her mother and father were US-born of Irish parents but had no recollection of any of her grandparents. Schooling ended for her at the age of nine when her mother died. By the age of sixteen she was married, a good marriage that would last over fifty years until the death of my grandfather. She had clearly and deliberately left the sorrows and disappointments of her childhood behind her and made a clean break with her own family, the history of which she knew very, very little. With her marriage, Kate joined her husband's large, loving family and walked forward to become a great mother, wonderful grandmother, and great-grandmother in her own right.

I am the only daughter of Kate's only daughter, Arlene. My mother had five brothers, all now deceased. They were a close-knit family (save for one brother who willingly estranged himself once he married), and my uncles and my aunts (their wives) were a wonderful part and constant of my own life. As their numbers have dwindled in my adult years, I feel the loss of their "chain links" anchoring me. I am fortunate to still have my mother and three aunts and treasure their continuing presence as my own link "weathers" with the passing years.

My mother, observing my closeness to my grandmother, once remarked without jealousy or implied criticism that I might love her mother more than her. My reaction was matter-of-fact and instinctive: the right word was not "more," it was "differently." A mother's being is fused with that of her child from the moment of conception, and when her baby emerges from the shelter of her womb and takes a first independent breath, a mother embarks on an incredible journey with that child for the next two decades. That journey is at times wonderful, awful, exhilarating, draining, and it goes on day after day after day. A mother knows the naked truth, literally and figuratively, about her child and has to cry foul when the child she loves strays or disappoints. I remember one of my sons launching into a teenage tirade that ended with the words "I can't stand you" ("can't stand" being code for "hate," I suspect). Such is life, and love, for a mother. A grandmother who has put in her time in that "mother" role, when rewarded with a grandchild sees that child not in the harsh light of that naked truth but rather through a lens that focuses on the grandchild's best traits and attributes. As for the child, what could be better than that? I can't think of any circumstances that would result in that son of mine telling his grandmother that he can't stand her.

I am reminded of a story my mother loves to tell about an "incident" when I was about two years old. My mother planned a treat for me: an outing to New York City for some holiday shopping and a visit to Santa Claus at Macy's on 34th in Manhattan. I was decked out in my tweed dress-up coat with the velvet trim and matching hat. Apparently, I am told, I was a perfect brat the entire day, impossible to please or placate even with the purchase of a lovely little pocketbook to go with my spiffy outfit. I allegedly cried my way through the streets of New York, whipping myself into a veritable frenzy. The obligatory visit to Santa did take place, complete with a black-and-white photograph to remember it by. God, I love that photo. It may be the best photo ever taken of me…ever. Santa looks as real as Kris Kringle, the Macy's Santa in the movie *Miracle on 34th Street*. I am looking straight into the camera lens, eyes like sad saucers, no smile but no tantrum either and no tears that I can see. And, I am holding that brand-new pocketbook.

My mother recalls getting me home and all but "throwing" me in my crib after the day from hell. I suspect that, in keeping with my signature perversity, I was pretty pleased to put my head down in the comfort of my own bed and take a nap after my misadventures of the day. The good news for my mother was that we were not, at that time, living with my father's Italian parents. If we were and my mother had zoomed into the house, scolding me for being bad and then "escorting" me to the crib, my grandmother Emanuela would likely have had an apoplectic fit, complete with expostulations of *"mio dio, mio bambino,"* arms waving in a torrent of Italian gesturing, a perfect illustration of motherly versus grandmotherly viewpoints.

My grandmother Kate, as I daringly and teasingly called her sometimes, was born in 1904 in Jersey City, New Jersey. Like her mother, she was an Irish redhead and, also like her mother, had something of the fiery nature often stereotypically associated with those copper tresses. When I repeatedly asked her about her childhood and her Irish roots, she reacted with surprise that I (or anyone) would be interested in that and saying, "It was all in the past and doesn't matter anymore."

In the mid-1970s, I was young, married, and the mother of my firstborn son. I stopped working when he was born and, in contemplating my new role as the primary caregiver and moral role model for the helpless innocent he was, I suddenly felt the full weight of responsible adulthood bearing down on my shoulders. It was a daunting prospect. Luckily for me (and for him), my two best pals were my mother and her mother…just the maternal support system I needed. My grandmother, recently widowed, came down on the "Red and Tan" bus from Jersey City to stay with my divorced mother most weekends. On Saturdays we food-shopped together and cruised the Kresge 5&10 store where my son invariably got a Matchbox car or some other treat from his Nanny or Great-Nanny.

Those weekend visits were the times when I asked my grandmother about her early years and family. It was also the time when I began to take my first stabs at trying to research our Irish family lineage. In those ancient pre-computer days when the Internet was still just a twinkle in Al Gore's mind's eye, research meant paper requests and communication via the US Post Office, then the only game in town. On the positive side, copies of official documents like birth, marriage, or death certificates were thankfully available at a very nominal cost, which meant I could afford to "dabble" now and then. Since no one had ever heard of "identity theft" or "terrorism," access to those documents was pretty much open to any and all. Those were also the days before Jersey City, the historic hub of my Irish family, became the poster child for official document corruption when municipal vital records staff were found to be selling fake birth records to those who could pay their asking price.

Over cups of tea at my kitchen table, I hung on every word, every story my grandmother told me. As I was pouring one of those cups of tea, she paused in telling me her story to point out that the "arse-end" of my kettle needed cleaning. She was a fastidious homemaker who changed her curtains four to six times a year and she wasn't shy about pointing out the occasional cobweb comfortably resting behind my kitchen curtains. As I listened to her tell the story of her childhood, writing down everything she told me, I passionately promised her that I would find out about her Irish roots and solve the mysteries of her family past. My promise was most sincere, if not kept in her lifetime. A feisty, spirited charmer when I hosted her 75th birthday party at my home, by eighty she had fallen into the rabbit hole of Alzheimer's and agonizingly slipped away, descending to a cruel death at the age of eighty-three, no longer knowing any of us, including me.

Three decades and much digging later, I have carefully darned together the fragments of her life, including the story of her Irish roots back to the late eighteenth century in the west of Ireland. I now know, as I suspected, that she hadn't told me everything...

at least I believe I found out things about her childhood that I do think she would have known but did not share with me and I understand why. The shattered pieces of life can draw blood and leave a scar...or as Daniel Patrick Moynihan once said: "To be Irish is to know that in the end the world will break your heart."

CHAPTER 1

A Promise Kept

Dear Kate,

Nearly three decades ago, I made a promise to you. While my earnestness and zeal in making the promise remain vivid in my memory, equally clear is my recollection that you never sought the promise and, in retrospect, may very well not have wanted it. I am certain you saw the sincerity of my pledge and its importance to me and, whatever your own feelings, "accepted" it on that basis the way one does for someone they love. In doing that for me, did you know that the promise and, ultimately, the long journey born of it were rooted in my love and admiration for you? Pride is an emotion that can generate powerful waves of motivation and, if misdirected, great destructive forces. But pride doesn't always, as the saying goes, precede a fall nor should it always be associated with the darker aspects of human behavior. Personal pride that is not self-directed but is born of admiration of another with whom we are linked in our hearts or minds is something very different. It can simply be called "pride by association," I guess. Kate, did you recognize the pride by association that was the seed of my promise to you? Just to be sure there is no chance of misunderstanding, I was and I remain proud of you and the story that is yours, and so mine.

They say that some things are well worth waiting for. The story I have to tell you is that and more in my view. The "more" aspect involves the tale of how the story was discovered in small revelations, subtle clues, surprising twists and turns on the road of research, unraveled mysteries, and ultimately in slowly darned holes in time and the piecing together of the fabric of a humble but long-lasting family lineage. Together, the "story" and its "tale" are the proverbial "whole" that is greater than the sum of its parts. So, it is going to take awhile for me to tell you everything I want and need to tell you, so please bear with me, humor me if you must, but just come with me on this journey…all the way to the end. No, that's wrong. Come with me all the way to the beginning.

About that story of yours: I can picture you reading the above and hear you saying, "What **story**? I never went past the fourth grade because my mother died of the consumption and my father then joined the Army and left us. We kids were separated and farmed out to different relatives. Why do you want to know about that? It was such a long time ago and doesn't matter anymore. You shouldn't take skeletons out of the closet. Why would you care about that anyway?" I heard you say those words more than once as I teased out your memories over a cup of tea at my kitchen table all those many years ago. I still have the now-tattered notebook where I wrote down everything you told me… albeit sometimes reluctantly. Its pages were like a peek through a keyhole and without any conscious thought or hesitation, I knew I had to find the key and open that door to me and so to you. And hence the promise, the unsought pledge to find the key, open wide the door to the past and re-knit past to present, whatever the discoveries, whatever the joy, whatever the sadness. Well, Kate, better late than never, it's time to keep that promise.

I have been trying to decide where to start. My first thought was to go straight to what I now consider the "beginning" and then walk forward with you, neatly connecting moment to moment with fine stitches and ultimately creating a delicate life's doily just like those you crocheted so many years ago. Then I wondered if it might be better to travel backward in time from your childhood on the winding paths that would bind us, place to place, person to person, generation to generation. Truth be told, your story has been discovered bit by bit, disjointed piece by disjointed piece, in no particular chronological order and according to no neatly orchestrated plan or schematic. I suspect I will recount it in the same fashion and hopefully with the same sense of "ooooh and aaaah" amazement and excitement that came with each original discovery. Since I am the guide for this odyssey, for better or worse, this is what we will do. No GPS. (Do you know what GPS is?) No itinerary. Despite the much-delayed timing of our journey and my nearly overwhelming feeling of urgency to tell you everything, there is no reason to rush and there is every reason to savor each morsel and be touched by every aspect whether joyful or tragic, tender or raw.

For what must be the hundredth time, I am looking at the only photo I have of you as a young woman, a young mother, barely twenty years old. You are not smiling. You look straight into the camera, unflinchingly. What are you thinking? Who is behind the camera? The photo is black and white of course but I "see" your wavy red bobbed hair just the same. You look a bit the "flapper" with your gauzy drop-waist dress with slit sleeves and embroidered neckline and skirt. Your dark strapped pumps match the purse you hold casually at your side. A short strand of pearls rings the base of your neck. Who gave you those pearls I wonder? What occasioned the photograph? I imagine that it is a Sunday and perhaps you are going to church. No, not church, that dress is not a "church dress"...not with those slit sleeves and shoulder tops peeking out. As countless times before, I take in how lovely you look and wish I had even one other photo of you as a child, adolescent, or young woman so I could put them side by side and examine every tiny aspect and from that darn the holes of time and history, filling them in with the threads of my intuition. Yes, I said "intuition," not imagination. I am not imaginative in the least but I am, I have discovered over the years, a natural intuiter. The unspoken, the nuances, the whisperings in the background noises of daily life, I hear them and moreover, I "see" them in that they are part of the context of my experiences. Some might call it ser-endipity when things come together, or fate. I believe it is just a different level of perception that some people have and that only some of those same people recognize. In the past, I might have said that as I aged, the intuitiveness got *stronger* but, the truth is more likely that as I am aging, the static of daily life continues to diminish, and those whispers and nuances are more readily recognized. Moreover, at a point in time when I am experiencing a new level of personal clarity in my life, I am no longer passive toward them.

So, Kate, in mapping out our journey and encountering these holes in time and history, I have employed those intuitive road signs and you need not worry that we will become lost. You see, we once were lost. One could say we were lost to time, lost to history, but that is no longer so. Speaking of lost in time, do you remember that day many years ago when we went to church but no one was there? There we were, all proper, standing on the sidewalk in front of the church wondering where everyone was. Then we realized that the clocks had been pushed forward an hour overnight for the start of daylight savings time…but not ours! I guess my then-youthful intuitive skills were not working well that day.

CHAPTER 2

So Close But So Far Away

Kate, will you be surprised when I tell you that I can now, after thirty years of sporadic but relentless persistence, take you back to the Emerald Isle and Irish family roots that span more than two hundred years? Do I hear a faint "oooooh"? No matter how many times people fall captive to hearing me tell the story of my various discoveries, the tale comes out with great excitement and pride, as if it were the very first telling. You will remember how little there was to work with, how little you knew. You will also no doubt remember my limited successes during the 1970s and 80s in unearthing some family marriage, birth, and death records for your Aunt Annie, your sister Mary, and mother Mamie and some bare-bones information about your father Patrick's service in the US Army. They were the tiny morsels that fed my curiosity and sustained the optimism that motivated me and made me believe I could and would succeed in my search.

I remember that dreary, drizzly, overcast day when we discovered your mother's unmarked grave at Holy Name with the clarity usually reserved for some very special life event. It would not be the last time I stood at her grave. The second time, some thirty years later, the sky would be clear blue and the only moisture would be tears I could not hold back, overflowing from my eyes. I lifted my chin to the heavens in an effort to try and keep the tears at bay and instead felt the warmth of the late summer sun drying my damp cheeks. I wish you had been there with me. I console myself with the belief that when you left us, you were freed from the cruel grip of the Alzheimer's that had stolen you from us piece by piece, day by day, and memory by memory. It sounds trite but I know with certainty that you are with me and I easily (and often) conjure up a mental video of you in a whoop of laughter, arms flying up across your chest.

By 1990, although up to my neck in children and career, I was still dabbling, looking for new leads and information sources. You know what they say: if you want something done, give it to a busy person. I had gone back to college at night to become a paralegal, which had led to my first position in a large local commercial bank. I joined the bank's commercial real estate lending department, assisting with the closing of large multimillion dollar loans to real estate developers and investors. One colleague would later describe the lending climate in those days as akin to opening the sixth story windows of the bank headquarters and throwing cash out of those windows to be caught by eager developers holding large wash baskets on the sidewalk. Not long after starting with the bank, in my naiveté, I questioned the way something was handled. One of the bank officers in our group explained the "golden rule" (which I thought I already knew) to me: "Them that have the gold, make the rules." As it turned out, I had joined the bank just before everything "hit the fan" and there were billions of dollars of "everything," trust me. This event is now remembered as the early 1990s real estate banking credit crisis or more colorfully as the S&L (savings and loan) collapse. I remember it as the start of what would turn out to be a pretty damn good twenty-plus-year career for me. But, I digress...

That dabbling I mentioned included learning that Irish surnames (like Flannelly and Whalen) were generally associated with specific regions or counties in Ireland, meaning that, in the absence of even the foggiest idea of family origin in the old country, those geographical surname ties could significantly reduce the size of the haystack containing my "needle." The surname Whalen, already complicated by the interchangeable and more common spelling "Whelan," had multiple regional ties in Ireland. Not a good start. The name Flannelly, however, was firmly rooted in two adjoining counties in the west of the Republic of Ireland, Mayo and Sligo. At that time, I was ignorant of the fact that the name Flannelly had its origins in pretty much the same root system as the name "Flannery." That ignorance was, in retrospect, a good thing as it kept me focused on Mayo and Sligo and I was not distracted or discouraged by the tangents that would have arisen from dealing with the Flannery effect. Acting on my newly found lead, on September 2, 1990, I wrote a letter addressed (literally) to the "Local Parish Priest, Sligo, Ireland." A Canon James Gilvarry of Easkey, County Sligo, kindly responded to my inquiry just ten days later. Luckily, perhaps in the spirit of economy, he penned his response at the bottom of my letter and I still have that original correspondence with his kind reply as follows:

"Dear Reverend Father,

For many years I have been trying to trace the ancestry of my dear grandmother. I have had almost no success as she was raised like a foster child and was separated from her siblings in the process. I always promised her that I would find out where in Ireland her people originally came from. She fell ill with Alzheimer's disease about six years ago and died two years ago. Although I could not keep my promise during her lifetime, I have not given up on it. I am writing to you in the faint hope that your parish records may hold the key to the information I have been seeking. I am given to understand that my great-grandmother's family name FLANNELLY is common to your area. That is why I am reaching out to you.

It is my belief (but I don't know it to be a fact) that my great-great-grandparents were immigrants who were born in Ireland in the 1840s. The dates and names as I know them are as follows:

John Flannelly – Born 1842 or 1843
His eventual spouse – Delia Hare – Born 1848 or 1849

I was not able to find a record of their marriage in the USA but I did find evidence of the birth of their children in Jersey City, New Jersey beginning around 1880.

Could you please check your records as to whether or not my great-great-grandparents are from your area? I would be most grateful.

Looking forward to hearing from you,
Maureen Wlodarczyk"

Canon Gilvarry's response:
"Easkey, Co. Sligo, 12–IX-90

Dear Maureen,

Sorry I can't be of any assistance; our books go back only to 1865. We have a Flannelly family here but they don't know of John Flannelly. You see, the Great Famine, 1845-47, disrupted all records and scattered our people to the ends of the earth.

With every good wish,
(Canon) James Gilvarry"

The Irish have the most beautiful way with words. I am not referring to the gift of gab or the fabled effect of puckering up to the Blarney Stone. There is a poignancy and poetry in their use of language. But there is also wry cleverness and sophisticated humor as well. It is born of and unique to their centuries of struggle for the freedom of their culture and the return of their lands and their perseverance to survive no matter what.

Canon Gilvarry's response of few but powerful words seemed to mark another dead-end, another failed attempt. My eyes took in his words: "the Great Famine...scattered our people to the ends of the earth," and they pricked me like a thorn in the pit of my stomach. The wound felt personal, very personal. In my mind I saw an image of seeds blowing in the wind at the mercy of events and forces that would determine if they would find fertile soil and regenerate or wither and die in unwelcoming sands. His words in their seeming finality were actually whispers of future discoveries. This would not be the last time I would cross paths with someone from Easkey during my searching and I would learn that the ill winds of the Great Famine did, in fact, scatter our seeds across the Atlantic.

After revisiting the Gilvarry letter, I found my thoughts drifting back, trying to put that isolated event of September 1990 into the context of my life in those days. Things were spiraling down at work. The real estate banking crisis was erupting like Vesuvius spewing a torrent of so-called bad loans. And with that came an onslaught of state and federal regulators, day in and day out, month after month, examining the aftermath of what they might have prevented. Isn't that what regulations are for...to provide the oversight and enforcement to preempt these things?

Six-day weeks and ten-plus-hour days were the norm as we paddled furiously to keep our collective heads above the rising tide of bad news and more bad news. Despite that, we bonded and banded together, rising to the occasion of every demand for information or explanation. Many of those who were in that "we" remain friends today nearly two decades later and, on those occasions when we cross paths personally or professionally, we still talk about those days with animation, laughter, and something very much like nostalgia. War stories of a sort. Ultimately, the bank would of necessity strip itself down, sell off assets, and finally deliver itself into the hands of a larger (and supposed wiser) financial institution but I was not there when the curtain came down. Like many others, worn down by the relentless pace and the struggle to find light at the end of the tunnel, I had gone looking for a new employer and had succeeded. In consideration of leaving colleagues and friends I respected and taking on a much longer daily commute, I would get a promotion to Vice President, a thirty-three percent salary increase, and a similar position in a much smaller and much healthier local bank. And she lived happily ever after...not exactly.

There is a framed photograph on the wall in our home office. I avoid looking at it because of the way I look and the memories it conjures up the minute I glance at it. I am not the subject of the photograph, just a spectator in a happy family event: a community swearing-in ceremony. My face is ashen white despite my rouged cheeks and lipstick trying valiantly to inject some color. My large brown eyes are hooded, cast down, and vacant in a way I don't recognize in the person I am today. I am fragile, pained, and holding on so tenuously, trying not to spoil the moment. This photo was taken not long after my job change.

My then new employer and new coworkers had no role in the slide I took when I changed jobs. I eventually came to understand that once I had stopped running through that tunnel looking for light, I forgot to step off the tracks before the approaching train hit me. All the adrenaline and purposefulness that had coursed through my veins for so many months dried up and drained away and the exhaustion came upon me at a time when I was made more vulnerable by the recent separation from those who had been a de facto support system in that dark tunnel. I felt generally sick, dizzy, and weak. I thought of asking for my old job back, thinking I had made a mistake in leaving, but I didn't do it. I had made a commitment to my new employer, who had generously offered money, status, and opportunity in a stable environment. Once I realized what was going on with me, I started to turn the corner and get back on track, no pun intended. Over the ensuing ten years, I would grow with that small bank and have the opportunity to become a senior manager and mentor, orchestrating my own successful career and working with many others to develop theirs. It was a life-changing decade despite the inauspicious beginning.

I try to avoid thinking of times in my life when I was struggling with a scary bout of illness like the one described above. My mother sometimes, even now, makes references to me not being "strong" or easily catching whatever is going around in the same way she would have done when speaking about me as a child. I know it is a form of concern or sympathy but no one likes to think they are "weak". Still, there is one episode of illness, childhood illness in fact, that has a very different effect when I recall it. Kate, do you remember the summer I was staying with you and Pop in Jersey City and came down sick? I recall feeling badly but that's not what has stayed with me all these years. In my mind I can still see myself lying in the middle of your big blond wood bed, all tucked in up to my chin. Then, in comes Dr. Front, beat-up black medical bag in hand, crouching down so he doesn't bump his head on the door frame. I felt so small in contrast to his long and lanky frame leaning over me, surprised but not scared. He pronounced me down with the "grippe." I still love saying it. Not a cold, not the flu. I had the *grippe!*

CHAPTER **3**

Traveling the Technological Highway

In the middle 1990s, the world of communication and information sharing and transfer was about to explode into its own version
of the Industrial Revolution. The tools, methods, and offspring
born of the research and development of this new technology,
in particular the "personal computer," were about to begin their
assimilation into the everyday lives of "regular" people at home
and in the workplace. How do I describe it? An enormous societal
change like the leap from radio to television might begin to give
a sense of it. A new way of storing information, sharing information, accessing information from third parties (the way you would
from a library), and the ability to communicate written material
via the airways from person to person, creating an alternate form
of paperless mail delivered in seconds around the globe. It is no
exaggeration to call it a proverbial cosmic shift, creating a new
norm for the approaching new century and something that would
throw open wide the door to accessing genealogical sources and
resources from one end of the world to the other.

Interest piqued, lively and inquisitive minds immediately began
identifying applications for this new technology and opportunities
to take it to the next level and the next. That continues to this day.
Among these creative ideas was the creation of a repository for
genealogical documentation such as US census records along

with birth, marriage, death, and military records, where professional and amateur family historians could research without ever
leaving their home...no matter where they lived.

It was during this time that I restarted my searching. Based on
the bits of Flannelly and Whalen Jersey City history I had kicked
up over the years, I concluded that your grandparents, John and
Delia Flannelly and Patrick and Kate Whalen, most likely married
in Jersey City in the years between 1865 and 1875. Searches of
marriage records for that period were available by request to the
New Jersey State Archives in Trenton. The search fee was nominal
and I decided to fill out the forms and give it a try. I tried not to get
my hopes up but with each day's mail, I became more anxious.
In a few weeks, a large envelope, worth its weight in gold, arrived
from the Archives. The conscientious and professional searchers
at the Archives found the marriage records for both sets of your
grandparents (my great-great-grandparents) and, even better,
those marriage registers included the names of the brides' and
grooms' parents (including their mothers' maiden names), reveal-
ing another generation! I was stunned and delirious with excitement and I wished you were with me to share in the discoveries.

While waiting for the results of the Archives search, I had started familiarizing myself with search avenues on my computer. Now
able to view resources from around the world, I came upon information about genealogical researching in Ireland through what
they call County Heritage Centers. For a fee, they would search
in specific counties in Ireland in an attempt to confirm a suspected relative's birth there. All of this could be done electronically
through the computer without so much as a phone call. When the
Archives information arrived, I pulled together my best estimate
of John Flannelly's birth year and provided that and his parents'
names (William Flannelly and Mary Lang Flannelly) to the Heritage Center in County Mayo, Ireland, Mayo being one of the two
counties where the Flannelly surname was predominantly found.
The search was unsuccessful and I had to decide if I wanted to

pay a second fee to have the Heritage Center in County Sligo search their records. I wavered only for a moment and ordered the Sligo search. When the search results popped up in my computer, I prepared for disappointment but instead I read the words that immediately set me hooting and hollering and then to tears: yes, they had found the October 1841 baptismal record for John Flannelly, son of William and Mary Lang Flannelly of Skreen and Dromard Parish, County Sligo, Ireland.

My fingers flew across the computer keyboard as I composed an email to friends and family that started as follows: "Ask me who I am. I am the great-great-great-granddaughter of William & Mary Flannelly of Skreen, County Sligo, Ireland."

After so many years of searching for our Irish roots, connecting back to Ireland and to Sligo and further to Skreen-Dromard Parish was very emotional for me. I cheered out loud from one end of the house to the other, cried tears of joy and wished with all my being that you could have been with me to share in the discoveries. I was salivating at the prospect of more revelations from the homeland.

For another fee, I had the Sligo Heritage Center send me the marriage record for your great-grandparents, William and Mary Flannelly, who were married in Skreen-Dromard Parish. I was also able to get confirmations of the baptisms of two more of their children in addition to that of your grandfather John. It would later turn out that William and Mary had four other children born in Ireland, although no birth or baptismal records were found during the Heritage Center searches. How serendipitous was it that your grandfather John was one of the children whose baptismal record survived? If it had not, I most likely would never have been able to definitively connect him back to the specific locality in Ireland from which he emigrated. I believe it was meant to be and had been patiently waiting to be discovered for a hundred and fifty years.

Rather than feeling my mission or calling was done at that point, my intuitive self was pushing forward, exploring all the new avenues for computer-based research. I signed up for a free two-week trial offer for Ancestry.com, a computer-accessible genealogical forum with hundreds of thousands of historical records such as immigration records, ship passenger lists, US census records, military records, copies of obituaries and other newspaper articles, state-based birth, death and marriage records, and even international records of the same types. It was powerfully addictive. I was on it day and night into the wee hours. With every small success, I was hungry to find more. Ultimately, I sprang for a one-year membership. It was a Christmas gift from me to myself.

Even during the holidays, I found time to tool around in Ancestry, learning about all it had to offer, including the ability to post messages on an electronic "bulletin board" where members could provide family information in hopes of connecting with another member researching the same family or an extension of it. There was also the ability to post a copy of your family tree and make that available to other members. Not only did I take advantage of the opportunity to let others know about my family search, I looked through the listings put up by other members searching for Flannellys and Whalens.

Within a week, I came upon a listing posted by a member working on the family of a Eugene Flannelly, who was married to a Minnie Hartman. Those names rang a bell. I pulled out my old trusty notebook and there it was in the notes I had taken down when you had told me about your family all those years ago. You had an Uncle Eugene Flannelly, your mother's brother, who had married a woman of German descent, Minnie Hartman. Minnie had a withered or crippled hand that she always kept hidden in the pocket of her apron. I used Ancestry's system for communicating with other members and sent a message to the person who had posted the information about Eugene and Minnie Flannelly. I explained that I thought we were likely related (and how) and asked if their Minnie had a disability. Within a day or so, a response came back through Ancestry. Yes, their Minnie had a disability, a crippled hand. There it was. Bingo!

We continued to exchange information over the following days and there was more good news. They had already connected with another member who was also related to Eugene and Minnie. Even better, both of them lived in the NY/NJ area. I could hardly contain myself. I was near desperate to meet them, total strangers or not. I invited them to my home and a few weeks later, a date was set. They turned out to be such nice, nice people and they were family, real flesh-and-blood relatives. We spent a wonderful day together sharing family stories, the results of our individual research, including successes and dead-ends, and exchanged photos and records, which I made copies of so that each of us had a full set of that precious information. That open and generous exchange and sharing of information filled gaps, answered nagging questions, and provided a tantalizing peek at possibilities for more discoveries in the form of an 1860s deed for a burial plot in the oldest Catholic cemetery in Jersey City: St. Peter's.

The St. Peter's cemetery deed, in the name of the 1864 purchaser, one William Flannelly, would blow a gaping hole in my finely tuned assumptions about your grandfather John Flannelly's emigration from Ireland to America. Using the conventional scenario typical to so many immigrants, I expected that your grandfather, a young child during the horrific potato famine of the late 1840s and one of those fortunate to have reached young adulthood despite severe privations, struck out at the age of plus or minus twenty years old determined to seek the much-talked-about "better life." That theory would have placed his time of arrival in America in the early-to-mid 1860s, just in time for the Civil War. In my searching, I happened upon a Civil War military record for a John Flannelly from New Jersey who served a three-year stint in the Union Army. Could he be "our" John Flannelly?

In the fever to find recruits for the mustering Union Army ranks in the early Civil War years, so-called "recruiters" regularly frequented the docks in New York, meeting incoming ships teeming with immigrant men to whom they offered bonuses and stipends to sign on the dotted line and join the armed forces of their new homeland. To those weary men, drained by the ordeal of weeks of prolonged confinement in the bowels of the ship's steerage class, stunned by the bustling docks and likely without a waiting job, the prospect of an "easy" fifty dollars must have been almost irresistible. I envisioned your grandfather having been "hooked" in just that fashion. Was he *that* John Flannelly? The answer would come…later.

CHAPTER 4

Ashes to Ashes, Time Stands Still

The St. Peter's cemetery deed, burning the proverbial hole in my pocket, was waiting, the Holy Grail or Pandora's box. In trying to learn more about St. Peter's Cemetery, I found out that it was long-closed (full up) and that the records for the cemetery were under the administration of Holy Name Cemetery (originally known as Hudson County Catholic Cemetery), the cemetery where your mother and father were buried. I called the office at Holy Name and started my interrogation of the person who answered. Is St. Peter's Cemetery open to the public? Yes…and no. Very limited weekly hours on Sundays or by appointment. Are there surviving early records for specific graves? Yes. Could they check a plot for me over the phone? Yes…and no. They agreed to look up the grave based on the information I read from the deed. They confirmed the grave purchaser was William Flannelly. Then, they cast out their line. I saw the tasty wiggling worm and I bit…hard. They hooked me. The grave was actually a plot of four adjacent graves and there were seventeen people interred in them…and almost all of them named Flannelly. For a fee of $105.00 (they charged "by the head") payable to the nice folks at the Archdiocese of Newark, they would send me a grave transcript listing all seventeen people with their dates of death and ages as listed on their records. I virtually ran to the post office to send off the request with their fee and about ten days later, the transcript arrived and, to me, it was worth five times what it cost…at least.

I studied it again and again, trying to take it all in, interpret what it was telling me, and realign my frame of reference. William Flannelly? Could that be John Flannelly's father, meaning that John did not set off alone to make his fortune in America? Seventeen family members in one set of graves, most interred from the 1860s to about 1910, including William himself and a Mary Flannelly, most likely John's mother. I mapped, dissected, theorized, and plotted, laying out the skeleton of a possible familial structure for the seventeen dear deceased. Then, I went back to revisit available immigration records with the new assumption that our Irish had arrived in America a full generation earlier than I suspected. I set out to prove (or disprove) that your great-grandparents William and Mary Flannelly had packed up their children and left for America as a family, possibly to escape starvation and looming death during the potato famine.

Misspelled names ("Hennelly" for "Flannelly," "Flansy" for "Flannelly," etc.) caused near-defeat and acute frustration for days and days as I pored over ship passenger lists and early US census records for 1850, 1860, and 1870. That precious cemetery deed saved the day, however, as it provided the probable names of more of William and Mary's children, particularly the boys and including one with a less common first name: Owen. Targeting the name "Owen" in my searches with various misspellings of "Flannelly," I found the "Hennelly" family, who were steerage passengers on the ship *Marmion*. Comparing the first names and ages of William and Mary "Hennelly" and their six children, I knew I had found them. The US census records for 1850, 1860, and 1870 absolutely confirmed the finding that the Flannellys had come to America as a family fleeing the devastation of the famine. I thought my heart would burst! That joy was almost immediately followed by a realization of what they must have suffered. And then once again, as when I read Canon

Gilvarry's words, I felt the sudden sharp prick in my belly and involuntarily held my breath.

I saw you in a dream last night. With all the excitement and satisfaction of having discovered your ancestral roots, one would have expected it to have been a sweet dream of animated story-telling. But it wasn't. It was less a dream and more the reliving of a very particular day at the nursing home where you spent your waning days. Those weeks and months were composed of virtu-ally indistinguishable dark days of acute sadness following one after another as in slow motion. No matter how hard we clung to you, how white our knuckles, how strong our grip, you faded away like a slowly disappearing apparition, a ghost of yourself, first no longer recognizing us and then mute, uttering not a word or sound. We faithfully came to visit with our diminishing expecta-tions of reconnecting with you. Well-intentioned friends consoled me with assurances that you "were not in any pain," "had no idea what was happening" and the like. I would say "thank you" and "I hope you are right" but there were times when I looked into your eyes, seemingly so detached, and felt them bore into me. I swore they were silently pleading with me: "I'm in here, I'm in here. Help me." I prayed you weren't in physical pain and unable to say so.

As the months passed without communication, we visitors would lapse into talking about you (how you looked, where did that bruise come from, where were your slippers) as if you were not there or were deaf. It was unintentional and simply the result of resigned acceptance that you had passed over into the last stages of Alzheimer's, were unaware of your surroundings, and would never speak to us again...until the day you said what actu-ally would be your last words. As we sized you up and compared notes, you blurted out in a terse, clear voice: "Shut up!" After the shock subsided, I felt a wave of shame and fear at the thought that we had hurt you so much that you had mustered every remain-ing bit of strength to momentarily free yourself from your prison to let us know you were "alive." Perhaps it was just an unrelated coincidence. Even as I prayed it was, I knew I would never know and never forget it.

My mother, acutely aware of the theories that Alzheimer's has hereditary implications, has now reached the age when you started to show the telltale signs. Mercifully, I can honestly say that your daughter shows no signs of it as far as I can see. She has mentioned to me that she would not like to end her days as you did, casually adding that she is looking to me to make sure that doesn't happen. Just as casually, I smiled and pointed out that I would not like to spend **my** final days in a jail cell, so we will both have to keep praying that when our time comes, we will exit suddenly and without drama in the throes of a peaceful night's sleep tucked into the cool, crisp sheets of our own beds. Getting the last word, she reminded me to keep it simple when her time comes and just plop her into a Hefty trash bag and roll her out to the curb. Enough said.

I know why you visited my dreams last night. Today is your birthday and not just any birthday. This would have been the day you became a centenarian. If you were here, you could have received a congratulatory birthday card from the President of the United States. No way. You wouldn't have had the slightest interest in greetings from the White House.

As I have done so many times before, I once again dragged a chair into my walk-in closet, climbed up on it, stretched precariously, and reached up to pull down the many albums of family photos. No matter how many times I am drawn to do that, it never disappoints. Sometimes now I take out a magnifying glass, trying to peer down into the photos, noticing little details like the jewelry being worn or trying to identify where a photo was taken by focusing in on the background beyond those who are the subject of the photo. Sometimes I will grab the phone and call my mother, hoping she will know or remember something that will satisfy my curiosity. She says it is getting harder for her to recall as the years go by.

The photos of your 75th birthday party at my house always draw me in. All those dear people assembled for that special occasion, leisurely sitting on lawn chairs in my backyard, so at home not because of my hospitality but because of their connection with one another. Being the guest of honor, you are in most of the photos but the expressions on your face tell different stories from photo to photo. In posed shots with my mother and then with me, there is a hint that you would rather not have complied…too much fuss. In another shot with your two sisters-in-law, who were more like actual sisters to you, you are at ease. Then there is the photo of you and your old, old friend "Begley" (Mrs. Begley to the rest of us). You are sitting and talking. Your chairs are not very close together and so you are both leaning in toward each other to close the gap. Rather than looking like two elderly ladies, the act of leaning in for some private conversation is reminiscent of two young girlfriends sharing something only for their own ears, something you two no doubt did decades earlier as young wives and mothers.

I am thinking how glorious it would have been to give you a 100th birthday party today. Instead, I am boiling (you would have said "burling") water for a cup of tea, which I will drink to you. Happy Birthday, Kate!

CHAPTER 5

In the Beginning

Having confirmatory evidence from both sides of the Atlantic Ocean that anchored the timeline of our Flannelly ancestors' no doubt reluctant flight from their Irish homeland, never to see it or those they left behind again, it was time to learn every damn thing I could about the Great Famine, a plague of nature that became, at the hands of the occupying English, the instrumentality of a veritable genocide against the indigenous Irish Catholic population.

I hunted down dozens of books on the subject of Ireland in the period during the Famine (1845-1850) and I devoured them. I was soon recounting what I had read to friends and family whether they wanted to hear it or not. From there, I moved on to Irish history in general with the same ravenous appetite. As I tell you our Irish family story, I mean to weave a background of context via a broad synthesis of what I have read and learned from those many fine works in hopes of breathing life and soul into the chart of our family tree. My discoveries solve our very personal mysteries; the scholarly works of these authors of the last two centuries bear witness to the tragedy and triumph of Ireland and all her people.

The more I read, the more I wanted to read and the more I felt joined to the Flannellys. I imagined and envisioned them trying to keep their children from starving, day by day, as conditions steadily worsened and there was nothing for it but to stay and face agonizing death from hunger or disease or literally walk out to a port town, board a ship, and survive a voyage of a month or longer crammed into the belly of a sailing ship, hoping to beat the odds and live to start over in America. They became, and remain, as real as any flesh-and-blood family I have ever known. But for their courage, there would be no "me" and no story to tell.

I was equally curious about the Jersey City they called home over a hundred and fifty years ago and dove into learning about its history as well. Yes, we have a century and a half intertwined with that community. I thought about the images of the Jersey City the Flannellys first saw; a "suburb" of New York, dotted with farms and not yet near becoming the industrialized community of its future. Contrast that with the Jersey City of your childhood at the turn of the twentieth century, the product of diverse ethnic immigration and the mechanization of factories and "horseless carriages." And then there is the Jersey City my mother knew. She still talks so fondly about the Jersey City of her youth and describes a wonderful place to grow up, a bustling, large urban community where she always felt safe.

A hundred years before those happy days of my mother's youth, her great-great-grandparents were integrating their family into the life of that city, immigrants clustering downtown with other Irish newcomers like themselves. Her feet and their feet no doubt literally trod some of the same streets and so did yours, a silent connectivity unrecognized by either of you. With deliberateness, I plan to walk those same streets as part of my journey "home." But now, it's time to go back to where the journey began: Doonflin Upper, Skreen, County Sligo, Ireland.

County Sligo, home of William and Mary Flannelly, is located in the northwest of the Republic of Ireland, not too distant from the border with Northern Ireland, which remains a part of the United Kingdom. Not to put too fine a point on it, Ireland is a small enough country that, in the context of distance as we view it in the expansiveness that is America, no place in Ireland is really "too distant" from most any other place.

On the whole, Ireland is unspoiled and lushly beautiful and its moniker, Emerald Isle, requires no explanation for those who have seen the place with their own eyes. Sligo, in the Province of Connaught, in its relative remoteness, is particularly unspoiled by "progress" and yet has the age-old character lines of the Ox Mountains and rugged shorelines sculpted by centuries of white-capped waves thrusting in from the Atlantic. There are irregular fingers of rocky coastline reaching out into the cool ocean, their weathered knuckles peeking through waterline, and beaches blanketed by the beading of smoothly polished pebbles. And yet, just beyond those stony shores lie expanses of the lush green emblematic of Ireland.

As for Skreen parish, records confirm the presence of the Flannelly name as far back as the fourteenth and fifteenth centuries, including multiple Flannelly men with the titles of Vicar or Rector of that parish. Doonflin Upper, a very small townland in Skreen, is where William Flannelly's name is found in an 1830s register listing tenant farmers. An Irish gentleman librarian in Sligo described Doonflin to me as a "wild place," meaning especially rugged terrain and very near those rough shores of the Atlantic Ocean described above. How challenging must it have been to tease out a living as a tenant farmer in such a place and to rely on it for subsistence with just enough left to cover the landlord's ransom for continued occupancy?

William Flannelly was born in about 1800 (some records indicate as early as 1798), the son of Owen and Mary Flannelly themselves born in Ireland in the last half of the eighteenth century. For Catholics, the eighteenth century in Ireland had seen them barred from the practice of their religion and stripped of all basic civil rights, including the right to hold public office and the right to own land under the Penal Laws of the period. Laws enacted for the specific purpose of institutionalized punishment and subjugation of Irish Catholics dated back to the late seventeenth century and Irish support for James II, a Catholic, in his battle to ascend the English throne. With his ultimate defeat came a series of laws designed to punish the Catholics of Ireland for supporting James II and to oppress the Irish Catholic population so severely that it could never again pose a threat to British Protestant rule. The Irish were stripped of the right to vote, practice law, or attend school. In effect, the Catholic Church was outlawed and the Irish turned to walking long distances to attend mass secretly in the open air in remote locations despite the threat of severe punishments if discovered.

A 1792 English geography text described the "old Irish" as "a miserable, depressed, and ignorant race, inhabiting the western and interior parts of the country." It goes on:

> "The present inhabitants are still represented as very ig-
> norant, uncivilized, and extremely apt to blunder both
> in discourse and behavior. They are very impatient of
> injuries, and apt to resent them in the most violent and
> outrageous manner; but are, notwithstanding that, very
> courteous and polite to strangers. In the Province of
> Connaught, they are more rude and barbarous than in
> other parts of the country. Their houses are only mean
> huts, composed of clay and straw, partitioned in the
> middle by a wall of the same materials; one end being
> appropriated to purposes of the family, and the other to
> the keeping of a cow… Their living is wretchedly poor,
> consisting of potatoes, coarse bread, eggs, milk, and
> sometimes fish. Their children are almost unacquainted
> with the use of clothes, and are commonly to be seen
> running about the roads stark naked. This extreme bar-
> barism is easily accounted for from the oppression which
> the common people undergo from their landlords; as
> well as the generality of them being Papists and kept

as much as possible in ignorance by their priests. The many disadvantages under which they have labored from their situation with the English government, have also contributed to the same purpose..."

And there we have the story of the long-suffering native Irish, replete with the de rigueur stereotypes of race, character, and religion, flawed and oppressed barbarians who remain courteous to strangers.

In truth, no matter how poor, persecuted, and systematically deprived of their civil rights and the basics of survival, Irish Catholics not only remained devoted to the practice of their religion, they kept faith with their culture, history, and desire for knowledge and education, especially for their children. Owen Flannelly and his son William may have attended so-called "hedge schools," illegal secret mobile gatherings where Catholic children received lessons from a Catholic teacher. Lord Palmerston, English viscount and absentee landlord of a large estate in County Sligo, is said to have written the following about his Sligo tenants:

"The thirst for education is so great that there are now three or four schools upon the estate. The people join in engaging some itinerant master; they run him up a miserable mud hut on the road side, and the boys pay him half-a-crown or some five shillings in a quarter. They are taught reading, writing and arithmetic, and what, from the appearance of the establishment, no one would imagine, Latin and even Greek."

Still, life went on as it must and always does and our William Flannelly, a damnable papist from that "crude and barbarous Province of Connaught," grew to manhood. On March 6, 1832, in the Roman Catholic Church at Skreen in front of witnesses Mary Flannelly and James Healy, William married Mary Lang, who was some dozen years his junior. Mary's parents were John and Abigail Lang, who married in Drung, County Cavan, Ireland in October 1808. Their marriage was recorded in the Church of Ireland, meaning that it was a Protestant marriage. Abigail Lang was born Abigail Leviston in Drung in January 1786. She was named for her mother, also named Abigail and the wife of James Leviston.

The Leviston surname, which has a number of variants including "Livingstone" or "Livingston," is most likely of Scottish derivation, as may be the name "Abigail," which is not at all a common Irish girl's name although it would be a name given to future female generations in our Irish family. Our Levistons may very well have been "Scots-Irish" who came to Ireland from Scotland as part of the Protestant "planting" encouraged by the English crown as part of its efforts to subjugate the indigenous Irish via intermarriage and achieve a resulting "dilution" of the native population.

Your great-grandparents, William and Mary Lang Flannelly of Doonflin Upper in Skreen, County Sligo, married just five months before the outbreak of a devastating cholera epidemic that would spare them but would take more than fifteen hundred of their fellow Sligoans in less than two months between August and September 1832. William and Mary would have seven children born to them between 1834 and 1845, two girls and five boys. The firstborn child, a girl named Eleanora, was born in January 1834 and was baptized in the same Skreen church where William and Mary were married. Twelve years later when the family would flee Ireland during the Famine, Eleanora was not with them. It is likely that she had died, perhaps in infancy or even during the early Famine period. In May 1835, a second daughter named Abigail (known as "Abby"), no doubt for her grandmother Abigail Leviston Lang, was baptized at the Skreen church in front of sponsors James Burns and Bridget Boland. After that there were five boys: Owen in 1837 no doubt named for his grandfather Owen Flannelly, Michael in 1839, John in 1841, Patrick in 1843, and Edward in 1845. John was your grandfather and my great-great-grandfather and he is the only one of the boys for whom there exists a baptismal record. He was baptized at the Skreen church on October 30, 1841 in front of witnesses Thomas Lang (perhaps Mary Lang Flannelly's brother) and Bridget Kilgallon.

In the first ten years of their marriage before the onset of the Famine, the Flannellys would have been building a life and a family in modest to meager circumstances. The 1833 government Tithe Applotment record describes the character of their small thirteen-acre plot of leased land as "arable," meaning suitable for plowing, sowing seeds, and raising crops. Those same records indicate William Flannelly leased that acreage from Jeremiah Jones, Esq. Jones' family had come to Ireland from their English homeland in the seventeenth century after the so-called "conquest" of Ireland by the forces of Oliver Cromwell. Cromwell, most well-known for successfully dethroning the British monarchy for a period in the middle seventeenth century, had then turned his forces toward a re-conquest of Ireland after a successful rebellion there several years earlier. He personally led those efforts with a legendary brutality. After subduing the Irish, whom he referred to as "barbarous wretches," Cromwell "dealt" with the Irish with a genocidal ethnic cleansing that saw thousands of native Irish men, women, and children transported or sold into slavery to work on plantations in the West Indies. In addition, he instituted his infamous "To Hell or Connaught" forced relocation of Irish landholders to the most remote, untamed lands in the country, awarding the lands confiscated from them to English gentry and military as incentive to participate in the "plantation" of Ireland. Jeremiah Jones himself was born in Ireland and his family had lived there for the better part of two hundred years at the time that William Flannelly leased a plot of land from him, land forcibly taken from the rightful Irish owners, who could have been Flannellys themselves.

The 1837 publication *A Topical Dictionary of Ireland* by Samuel Lewis provides the following description of Skreen:

"Skreen, a parish, in the barony of Tyreargh, county of Sligo, province of Connaught, 5 miles (E.) from Dromore-West, on the road from Sligo (town) to Ballina, and on Ardnaglass harbor; containing 4,567 inhabitants. This parish was anciently called Knock-na-moile, and was granted by Tipraid, Chief of Hy-Fiachrii, to St. Columb: it obtained its present name from a shrine of St. Adamnan erected here. From its contiguity to the shore of the Atlantic, great facility is afforded of obtaining valuable manure: agriculture is very bad, the peasantry being averse to adoption of any improvements, though the land itself is good; there is some bog in the mountains. At Ardnaglass is a good limestone quarry, from which some of the hewn stone work of the new chapel at Ballina was procured; it bears the chisel well and takes a good polish... Leckfield is the residence of Lewis G. Jones, Esq; Seafort, of R. Wood, Esq.; and Tubberpatrick, of Jeremiah Jones, Esq...The R.C. (Roman Catholic) parish is co-extensive with that of the Established Church, and contains a chapel... The old castle of Ardnaglass of which there are considerable remains, was originally the residence of the ODowds, a family then of great note... It is now the property of J. Jones, Esq., whose ancestor came over with Oliver Cromwell..."

I would say the Jones family did very well for themselves by riding into Ireland on the magic carpet of Oliver Cromwell's coattails and more to their credit may have helped give rise to the now familiar adage about "keeping up with the Joneses." Ultimately though, Jeremiah (Jeremy) Jones, who served as a Sligo magistrate, Grand Jury member, Sligo County Deputy, and chairman of the local Fever Hospital, would have his own troubles. His estate was put into receivership in the early 1830s and his estate home, Tubberpatrick House in Skreen, was sold in 1852. He took up residence on Stephen Street in Sligo Town and remained in that home until his death in 1875 at the ripe old age of eighty-five.

On those thirteen acres where William and Mary Flannelly and their children lived, there would have been a very modest cottage of one or perhaps two rooms built of locally found stone or mud-walled with a thatched roof. The cottage would have few, if any, window openings, and any windows would likely have been unglazed, no glass panes. The cottage would have been white-washed with a mixture made by burning local shells. There may have been a chimney opening in the thatched roof if they could afford the extra taxation assessed for having one. A turf or peat fire would be burning in the small hearth with a kettle of potatoes on the boil and the room would be bathed in a sheer blanket of trapped smoke slowly finding its escape to the outdoors. Turf was used for cooking and for heat and was taken from the local bogs, cut out in the shape of bricks, and then dried for later use. If the Flannellys were so fortunate as to own a pig or cow, that prized beast would have shared home and hearth with his owners. I envision a lively household with so many young children and so many adventurous little boys. The older children would have of necessity worked in the fields alongside their parents and helped with chores inside. The landlord must be paid timely as the threat of eviction for the slightest infraction, real or fabricated, followed like a dark shadow. The family's Roman Catholic faith, a fabric of their daily lives, would have defined them as "Popish," part of the underclass guilty of not recognizing the "true faith" of the English. In January 1839, the young family would have experienced the legendary "night of the big wind," a hurricane of a storm that uprooted great trees, hurled them like twigs, and literally blew houses down in a fury of gale winds, driving rain, and sea spray.

The Ordnance Survey Memoirs of Ireland, Volume 40 for the Counties of South Ulster 1834-38, included a section on County Sligo and the "Habits of the People" that described cottages "mostly built of stone," with "6, 8 and 10 houses clustered together on many townlands," "possessed by cottiers weaving coarse linen and woolen cloth"...and "renting as much land by conacre as will raise a sufficiency of potatoes for their sustenance." It went on to say:

> "Potatoes and milk in the season form the principal, and almost only, support of the population. Turf is generally free to the tenantry and the only fuel burned in the parish. Six is given as the average number of a family and, although great poverty and destitution oppress the people, many cases of great age are observable amongst them. No decided peculiarity of dress characterizes the population of the parish. The red cloaks and red petticoats of Connaught, so generally worn in Mayo or Galway, are occasionally observable on fair days and Sundays..."

Although the life-altering potato blight and accompanying Great Famine would not arrive until late 1845, during the preceding decade many of the Irish peasantry lived tenuously, eking out one day at a time, keeping just out of the grasp of starvation and eviction by means of the charity of some of their neighbors who were only slightly less vulnerable than those they tried to help.

Two French noblemen, Alexis de Tocqueville and Gustave de Beaumont, journeyed to Ireland in the mid-1830s for a six-week tour of the country related to a larger study of the societal and political climate in the British Isles. These two men in their mid-thirties had already visited the United States observing the American political system, both having a strong interest in the ongoing movement from aristocracy to democracy around the world. They documented the shocking Ireland they found in stark vignettes of awful truth, Tocqueville in his journal notes and Beaumont in his 1839 *Ireland: Social, Political and Religious*. Tocqueville's notes from late July 1835 recount a conversation with a local Catholic priest during which he asked if the priest would agree that the Marquis of Sligo, having returned to his local estate to find the "extreme distress" of his own tenant farmers, would now take steps to relieve that distress. The priest's reply, in all its succinct and painful clarity, as recorded by Tocqueville:

"You must be very ill informed about the state of Ireland to ask me such a question, said the priest. Do you not know the aristocracy is the cause of all our miseries and that they do not alleviate any of the evils that they give rise to? Do you not know what prevents the poor man from dying of hunger in Ireland? It is the poor man. In Ireland, it is the poor who provide for the needs of the poor, it is the poor who raise and maintain the schools where the children of the poor are brought up, it is the poor finally who furnish the poor with the means of obtaining the comforts of religion. A farmer who has only thirty acres and who gathers only a hundred bushels of potatoes, puts aside a fifth of his harvest annually to distribute to those unfortunates who are the most in need. The starving man presents himself without fear at the door of the thatched cottages; he is sure to receive something to appease his pressing hunger. But at the door of the mansions he will meet only liveried lackeys or dogs fed better than he, who will drive him harshly away. In order to give alms the farmer will spare the manure for his field, he will wear rags, his wife will sleep on straw, and his children will not go to school. What does the lord do during all this time? He strolls in his vast estate surrounded by great walls. In the enclosure of his park everything breathes splendor, outside poverty groans, but he does not notice it. He has big and fat dogs and his fellow creatures die at his door. Not only does he not relieve the needs of the poor in any way, but he profits from these needs by drawing enormous rents and goes to spend in France or Italy the money thus acquired. If he returns for a short time among us, it is to evict from his estate a farmer who is behind in his rent and evict him from his dwelling..."

Beaumont wrote as follows:

"I have seen the Indian in his forests, and the Negro in his chains, and thought, as I contemplated their pitiable condition, that I saw the very extreme of human wretchedness; but I did not then know the condition of unfortunate Ireland. Like the Indian, the Irishman is poor and naked; but he lives in the midst of a society where luxury is eagerly sought, and where wealth is honoured. Like the Indian, he is destitute of the physical comforts which human industry and the commerce of nations procure; but he sees a part of his fellows enjoying the comforts to which he cannot aspire. In the midst of his greatest distress, the Indian preserves a certain independence, which has its dignity and its charms. Though indigent and famished, he is still free in his deserts, and the sense of this liberty alleviates many of his sufferings: the Irishman undergoes the same destitution without possessing the same liberty; he is subject to rules and restrictions of every sort: he is dying of hunger, and restrained by law; a sad condition, which unites all the vices of civilization to all those of savage life. Without doubt, the Irishman who is about to break his chains, and has faith in futurity, is not quite so much to be bewailed as the Indian or the slave. Still, at the present day, he has neither the liberty of the savage, nor the bread of servitude."

"I will not undertake to describe all the circumstances

and all the phases of Irish misery; from the condition of the small farmer, who starves himself that his children may have something to eat, down to the labourer, who, less miserable but more degraded, has recourse to mendicancy—from resigned indigence, which is silent in the midst of its sufferings, and sacrifices to that which revolts, and in its violence proceeds to crime. Irish poverty has a special and exceptional character, which renders its definition difficult, because it can be compared with no other indigence. Irish misery forms a type by itself, of which neither the model nor the imitation can be found anywhere else. In all countries, more or less, paupers may be discovered; but an entire nation of paupers is what was never seen until it was shown in Ireland. To explain the social condition of such a country, it would be only necessary to recount its miseries and its sufferings; the history of the poor is the history of Ireland."

Across the vast Atlantic Ocean, there was also recognition of the daily struggle of Ireland's peasantry for the barest necessities of life. American Asenath Hatch Nicholson, born in Vermont and descended of a Puritan line, was nurtured in the values of charity and religious tolerance by her parents. She wrote that as a child in New England, her father had told her, "Remember that the Irish are a suffering people; and when they come to your door, never send them away empty." Later, she would relate that when she was in the "garrets and cellars" of New York, she did become acquainted with the poor Irish there and saw with her own eyes that they were, just as her father had said, a suffering people. She had also heard about the natural beauty of Ireland and longed to visit there and "breathe the mountain air of the sea-girt coast of Ireland" and to meet those Irish in their own country towns and cottages. In 1844, she made that long-awaited trip and traveled to every Irish county (except Cavan) over the ensuing fifteen months, walking through the countryside as she went and typically staying with the local poor or clergy. She distributed bibles in English and the Irish language as she met Protestants and Catholics of various stations in her travels. Her journal of those travels from 1844 until August 1845 (just prior to the onslaught of the Famine), *Ireland's Welcome to the Stranger*, published in 1847, presents an unvarnished view of what she referred to as the "dark curtain of desolation and death" hanging over the "fair landscape" of Ireland, including an eerily prophetic statement that conditions were such that "an explosion must soon take place...and Ireland be turned inside out." Still, she saw and noted the natural beauty she had so anticipated. County Sligo was among the places Asenath visited during her travels and she expressed regret at not being able to remain there longer, describing the view of the Bay of Sligo: "Here are mountains of rock, standing out in circular shape, with the appearance of pillars, as if hewn by an architect;...the little islands in the river, the green meadows and tasteful demesnes upon the border made an indescribable treat as the sun was setting." She also wrote of walking out some miles into the Sligo countryside, stopping in at a small cottage where she was kindly welcomed and invited by the inhabitants, who might have been our own Flannellys, to share their breakfast of brown bread and milk.

On the last page of *Ireland's Welcome to the Stranger*, she addressed Irish Catholics as follows:

> "To the Roman Catholics, both duty and inclination require that I should acknowledge a deep debt of gratitude. They have opened the doors of convents, of schools, of mansions, and cabins, without demanding letters (of introduction or recommendation), or distrusting those that were presented. They have sheltered me from storm and tempest; they have warmed and fed me without fee or reward, when my Protestant brethren and

sisters frowned me away. God will remember this, and I will remember it."

Asenath Nicholson would return to Ireland during the Famine from 1847 to 1848, spending a winter in the west of Ireland to organize relief for the poor in those most severely impacted areas, including Sligo. In a curious coincidence, she traveled back to America in 1852 and took up residence in Jersey City, once again creating the possibility of crossing paths with our Flannellys on the other side of the Atlantic. She died in Jersey City, stricken down by typhoid fever, in May 1855.

Despite the oppression and deprivation of many centuries, the native Irish never abandoned their faith in God, their love of family, or their struggle for freedom. Risings against the English occupiers repeated as new generational Irish leaders rallied their fellow Irish using political means and outright rebellion in an effort to regain basic civil rights, economic access, and political participation, if not full independence from England. As the 1840s unfolded there was another reigniting of the movement for Irish political indepen-dence in the person of Daniel O'Connell, who would come to be known as "The Liberator" for his ground-breaking inroads toward Irish self-determination. O'Connell even made his way to Sligo, in the mid-1840s before the onset of the first year of the failure of the potato crop, for what was called a "Monster Meeting," a demonstration of support for the Irish nationalist cause and "re-peal of the union" with England. Newspapers of the day described throngs of waving and cheering supporters on the Sligo roads as "The Liberator" traveled around the county. Perhaps William and Mary walked out to the road from Ballysodare to the town of Sligo, joining the crowds trying to catch a glimpse of Daniel O'Connell as his coach passed by that exciting day.

CHAPTER 6

Sligo Is No More

In general, daily life for the Flannellys prior to the onset of the Famine would have been hard but not without a thread of predictability, structure, and basic expectations. With the dispossession of the native Irish from their own land holdings, they became forced tenant farmers on plots of land generally of five to fifteen acres at most and sometimes as small as just a quarter-acre. As their sons came of age and married, that acreage was often parceled out to those sons, which had the effect of further increasing the density of population living off that limited land. Potatoes became the preferred crop for the most practical reasons: yield per acre and nutritional subsistence. The cultivation of those essential potatoes and a few other crops such as turnips was a year-long process using just a few rudimentary tools like spades and rakes. Tenant farmers rarely had ploughs or the horses to pull one. The land had to be turned and prepared with ridges for planting, and with the arrival of spring, the actual planting would be done. During the summer months, there was weeding to be done and the ridges had to be maintained to insure proper growth of the potato plants. By October, the potato harvesting was underway with the whole family working together, digging, sorting, and storing the crop for future use. It has been said that a single acre of potatoes could support an average Irish family for a full year, feeding the family and allowing for excess to be sold so rent and basic necessities could be satisfied.

There had been sporadic events of crop loss in the early nineteenth century that caused hardship for those who could least afford it but nothing like the perfect storm of the Great Famine of 1845-1850. The potato blight first appeared in the autumn of 1845 in Ireland when potato plants suddenly began turning black, literally rotting. Potatoes were quickly dug up looking healthy but then turned, a day or two later, to black foul-smelling mush. The cause of the blight, unknown at the time, was a fungal disease most likely transported to Ireland in the holds of ships arriving from North America. Wetter than normal weather in Ireland provided favorable conditions for the fungal spores to spread across the island, unfettered and rampant. With only about one-third or less of the crop surviving the initial attack of the blight and no other source of food or income, the Irish people struggled through the winter of 1845-46, praying that the potato crop in 1846 would be healthy.

The English government, despite alarming reports about the conditions of the Irish peasantry from various quarters including their own gentry, provided only some nominal temporary relief measures, which had little effect, particularly in the more remote areas of the West including Sligo. And, incredibly, Irish tenants were still expected to pay their rents to their landlords as required and those who could not were forcibly evicted. Tear-downs were the preferred method of removing tenants in arrears on their rent. Local officials would muster men to demolish the offending tenant's cottage using a battering ram or even burning it to the ground. Tenants were told to remove themselves not only from that property but also from the general area, a form of banishment. Formerly tenanted land was then repurposed by the landlords as grazing land for cattle, a more economically favorable arrangement for them.

There were prevailing views in London that Irish Catholics

were inherently lazy, unintelligent, slovenly, and generally inferior as a race and that to give them charity in the form of food would be to reinforce their negative character traits. They reasoned that the potato failure would not persist, might serve to teach the Irish not to be dependent on potatoes to live, and that the free markets would ultimately put things to right.

Neither the prayers of the Irish peasantry nor the laissez-faire attitudes of the English government would have any effect on the unholy societal plague that would be the An Gorta Mor, the Great Famine that would last some four more years, exterminating an estimated million Irish by starvation and disease as brutal evictions increased, and provoking an exodus of a million more Irish from their homeland in search of survival. Those who remained were reduced to walking skeletons, homeless, naked, wracked with dysentery, cholera, and typhus, which snuffed out the lives not taken by starvation. The Irish, subjects of England, then the wealthiest nation in the world, would wither, die, and decay in cruel metaphoric similarity to their lost potato crop while the English government "fiddled" in response. There is a word for what happened: holocaust.

In was in this time of unimaginable deprivation and hopelessness that William and Mary Flannelly found the courage and resolve to leave their homeland in an attempt to save their family. Their decision came in late 1846 with the confirmed catastrophic failure of the potato crop for the second year and the inevitable cascading of famine across all parts of the country. Where there had been hunger and privation, there would now be rampant starvation and its killing partner, disease, a reality so dire as to make William, a man in his mid-life forties, pull up ancestral roots, breaking with home and extended family to pursue more fertile ground in America.

Still, with singular arrogance and indifference the English government persisted in discounting the plight of the Irish peasantry while never stopping the exportation of foodstuffs from Ireland that could have been distributed to the starving population. The price of food that was available for purchase in Ireland sky-rocketed due to merchant gouging and hoarding. Some Indian corn was provided by the government but never in an amount or frequency that made a difference, nor did it provide any mean-ingful nutritional value. During the second year of the Famine, a public works project scheme was initiated, the idea harkening back to the view that getting food must be contingent on doing work. When the starving Irish heard about the works program, they queued up by the hundreds, an army of thin-skinned, skel-etal figures barefoot and in rags, men, women, and children ready to build unneeded roads or do whatever other hard labor was available in the hope of making some money to buy food. The works program was never expansive enough to employ more than a small portion of those who came forward to work, wages were in no way correlated to rising prices, and the projects were often canceled or stripped of funding without rhyme, reason, or explanation. In the midst of this abject failure to acknowledge or respond to the ever-worsening situation, some aid came from outside the British Empire. Native American Indians raised funds for Irish relief as did Irish-Americans, and the Society of Friends (commonly known as Quakers) came to Ireland to minister to Famine victims. The world could see what the English govern-ment could not or would not.

At the same time, many English gentry landlords, some absen-tee and others in residence in Ireland, applied their intellect and resources not to stemming the accelerating crisis or alleviating the daily suffering and death among their Irish tenants but instead to ridding themselves of the burden of those tenants. The so-called "Poor Laws" of the day assessed these landlords with a tax pay-able on behalf of their small tenant farmers, whether or not those tenants were able to pay their rent. The taxes paid were used to support local workhouses, which took in the poorest of the local Irish peasantry. As thousands of tenant farmers defaulted on their rent payments, landlords realized that clearing tenants from their estates offered both the advantage of escaping the poor tax and the freedom to repurpose the land as they chose.

Two methods were readily available to these landlords. First: swift and often violent evictions of tenants even nominally in arrears on their rent payments. The second scheme was more creative and insidious: "assisting" tenants to emigrate to the US or Canada by arranging for paid ship passage for tenant families. It has been said that the cost of buying those tickets was half of the amount it would have cost those landlords to keep their tenants in residence on their estates. County Sligo was a focus of this "assisted emigration," Sir Robert Gore-Booth of Lissadell in Sligo being infamous among the landlords who orchestrated these removals and emigrations.

Less than a decade earlier, Samuel Lewis's *Topographical Dictionary of Ireland*, in its description of the inhabitants of Sligo, commented on the locals' habits with respect to the waking of their deceased friends and neighbors.

> "The estimation in which a man has been held during his life is judged of by the attendance on these occasions and at his funeral: to be absent is therefore considered a serious offence, and much expense is incurred in procuring the necessary refreshments for the numbers that attend."

As the Famine increased its death grip in Sligo, the respect and dignity associated with dying fell victim to the desperate times, replaced by the expediency of reusable coffins with false bottoms and the reality of the dead lying on roadsides or in ditches where they fell and where their mortal shell would stay. The following contemporary poem by Oscar Wilde's mother tells it first-hand:

THE FAMINE YEAR (THE STRICKEN LAND)
By Jane Francesca Wilde

Weary men, what reap ye? — Golden corn for the stranger.
What sow ye? — Human corpses that wait for the avenger.
Fainting forms, hunger-stricken, what see you in the offing?
Stately ships to bear our food away, amid the stranger's scoffing.
There's a proud array of soldiers — what do they round your door?
They guard our masters' granaries from the thin hands of the poor.
Pale mothers, wherefore weeping — Would to God that we were dead;
Our children swoon before us, and we cannot give them bread.

Little children, tears are strange upon your infant faces,
God meant you but to smile within your mother's soft embraces.
Oh! we know not what is smiling, and we know not what is dying;
We're hungry, very hungry, and we cannot stop our crying.
And some of us grow cold and white — we know not what it means;
But, as they lie beside us, we tremble in our dreams.
There's a gaunt crowd on the highway — are ye come to pray to man,
With hollow eyes that cannot weep, and for words your faces wan?

No; the blood is dead within our veins — we care not now for life;
Let us die hid in the ditches, far from children and from wife;
We cannot stay and listen to their raving, famished cries —
Bread! Bread! Bread! and none to still their agonies.
We left our infants playing with their dead mother's hand:
We left our maidens maddened by the fever's scorching brand:
Better, maiden, thou were strangled in thy own dark-twisted tresses —
Better, infant, thou wert smothered in thy mother's first caresses.
We are fainting in our misery, but God will hear our groan:
Yet, if fellow-men desert us, will He hearken from His Throne?
Accursed are we in our own land, yet toil we still and toil;
But the stranger reaps our harvest — the alien owns our soil.
O Christ! how have we sinned, that on our native plains

We perish houseless, naked, starved, with branded brow, like Cain's?
Dying, dying wearily, with a torture sure and slow —
Dying, as a dog would die, by the wayside as we go.

One by one they're falling round us, their pale faces to the sky;
We've no strength left to dig them graves — there let them lie.
The wild bird, if he's stricken, is mourned by the others,
But we — we die in Christian land — we die amid our brothers,
In the land which God has given, like a wild beast in his cave,
Without a tear, a prayer, a shroud, a coffin or a grave.
Ha! but think ye the contortions on each livid face ye see,
Will not be read on judgement-day by eyes of Deity?

We are wretches, famished, scorned, human tools to build your pride,
But God will yet take vengeance for the souls for whom Christ died.
Now is your hour of pleasure — bask ye in the world's caress;
But our whitening bones against ye will rise as witnesses,
From the cabins and the ditches, in their charred, uncoffin'd masses,
For the Angel of the Trumpet will know them as he passes.
A ghastly, spectral army, before the great God we'll stand,
And arraign ye as our murderers, the spoilers of our land.

(Published for the first time as "The Stricken Land" in *The Nation*
23rd Jan. 1847)

It has been said that many of those who left in the early years
of the Famine before "Black 47," the single most devastating of
the Famine years as to loss of human life, were tenant farmers who
were in somewhat better financial circumstances than the average
and had the money and wherewithal to opt for emigration. Perhaps William Flannelly was one of "those" tenant farmers. Since
he didn't marry until his early thirties, he may have embarked on
married life after squirreling away some of his hard-earned coin.
Or perhaps, as a second winter without food was bearing down

on them, he looked into the eyes of his hungry children and, unable to see any other survival option, decided to sell their modest possessions in order to buy passage to America. One way or the other the decision so fateful for those of us who came after had been made.

CHAPTER 7

Out of Ireland

Ardnaglass, Skreen, County Sligo   *6ᵗʰ September, 1846*

Dear Father and Mother,
   I received your kind affectionate letter dated 24ᵗʰ May, which gave us great pleasure to hear of your being in good health, as it leaves us at present; thank God for his mercies to us. Dear father and mother, pen cannot dictate the poverty of this country, at present, the potato is quite done away all over Ireland, and we are told, all over prevailing Europe. There is nothing expected here, only an immediate famine. The labouring class getting only two stone of Indian meal for each day's labor, and only three days given out of each week, to prolong a little the money sent out by the government, to keep the people from going out to the fields to prevent slaughtering the cattle, which they are threatening they will do, before they starve. I think you will now have all this account by the public print before this letter comes to hand. Now, my dear parents, pity our hard case, and do not leave us on the number of the starving poor, and if it be your wish to keep us until we earn at any labour you wish to put us to, we will feel happy in doing so. When we had not the good fortune of going there, the different times ye sent us money; but alas, we had not the good fortune.

Now, my dear mother and father, if you knew what hunger we and our fellow countrymen are suffering, if you were ever so much distressed, you would take us out of this poverty Isle. We can only say, the scourge of God fell down on Ireland, in taking away the potatoes, they being the only support of the people. Not like countries that have a supply of wheat and other grain. So, dear father and mother, if you don't endeavor to take us out of it, it will be the first news you will hear by some friend of me and my little family be lost by hunger, and there are thousands dread they will share the same fate. Do not think there is one word of untruth in this; you will see it in every letter, and of course in the public prints... The Lord is merciful, he fed the five thousand men with five loafs and two small fishes...

This eyewitness testimony of conditions in Skreen Parish, with its painfully accurate prediction of what was to come, was written by one despairing father just weeks before the Flannellys left for America. At the same time, on the other side of the Atlantic Ocean, "The Irish Emigrant Society of New York," formed in 1841 for the express purpose of advising and assisting immigrant Irish, had published its updated annual message to those seeking refuge in America. The Society pulled no punches in delivering its guidance. Clerks, accountants, and "professional men" should not emigrate, as employment in those professions was scarce and preferentially awarded to US natives. They further discouraged relocation to the US eastern coast in general, suggesting instead that "laborers, mechanics...and those with some practical knowledge of agriculture" avoid the "Atlantic cities" in favor of settlement in the interior American territories. They pronounced that "the condition of the emigrant who remains in the Atlantic cities is very little, if at all improved" over their prior circumstances at home. The juxtaposition of these two views gives new meaning to being "between a rock and a hard place."

Emigration was a "process" and a daunting challenge from start to finish. First and foremost, money was needed to purchase tickets for both the short passage by ferry to the port of overseas embarkation and for the trans-Atlantic voyage to America. This usually meant emigrants would sell off whatever they could not or would not be taking with them for whatever price they could get from their struggling neighbors or local profiteers who hoped to buy at a pittance for resale later. In addition to having the money to purchase ship tickets, emigrants were responsible for carrying provisions to sustain them during the journey and some even brought their animals, especially pigs, with them. The shipping companies did distribute small amounts of bread, oatmeal, and water, often spoiled or contaminated, and certainly not an adequate diet in any event. Famine emigrants, already weak from hunger and often with barely the clothes on their backs, often fell prey to illness or death in their desperate attempt to make the voyage out of Ireland.

I often see our Flannellys in my mind's eye in a series of vignettes drawn from what I have read and from engravings of the day that I have collected over recent years. The wretched images in London newspapers of Ireland during the Famine years are etched into my subconscious and consciousness both. Sometimes, there is such clarity that I am almost projected into those scenes, willfully fusing myself into their world trying to "feel" what it was really like.

It was a crisp autumn morning in mid-October 1846, the last day the Flannellys would awake in Skreen...ever. They would have sought out their local priest for an all-important family blessing that God's mercy and providence would sustain them through their emigration odyssey. Where neighbors once routinely gathered together for so-called "emigrant wakes," rites of passage for those they believed they would never see again, the exodus was now so large and privation so severe as to all but snuff out such traditions. If our Flannellys were lucky, they had some type of primitive handcart on which they could put their belongings and provisions along with the youngest of the six children. Just as likely they did not and would have instead used their backs in substitute, taking turns carrying the youngest children in their arms.

As they walked out leaving their home for the last time, they tried not to look back but stole one quick glance over the shoulder. The first leg of their journey was the fifteen-mile trip to the Town of Sligo on foot. Sligo was an active port town where they would board a paddlewheel steamer for Liverpool, England, a trip of perhaps one and a half to two days. In their expansive three volumes titled *Ireland, Its Character & Scenery* (1841), Mr. and Mrs. S.C. Hall shared their observations about Irish emigrants preparing to depart from the port at Cork, a "band of two hundred exiles" surrounded by an "immense crowd" seeing them off and went on to say:

"The scene was very touching; it was impossible to witness it without heart-pain and tears. Mothers hung on the necks of their athletic sons; young girls clung to elder sisters; fathers—old white-headed men—fell upon their knees, with arms uplifted to heaven, imploring the protecting care of the Almighty on their departing children. Several passed bearing little relics of their homes—the branch of favourite hawthorn tree whose sweet blossoms and green leaves were already withered... It is impossible to describe the final parting. Shrieks and prayers, blessings and lamentations, mingled in "one great cry" from those on the quay and those on shipboard... Some, overcome with emotion, fell down on the deck... We heard a feeble voice exclaim, "Dennis, Dennis, don't forget your mother—your poor old mother!"

The steamer to Liverpool, a small ship, would have been crowded and teeming with people and animals. Two hundred souls were likely on board, including Irish paupers with no means who were going to Liverpool not as a first step in overseas emigration but as a final destination, hoping to find work or get on the relief rolls. These small vessels were without shelter, and passengers, already in a weakened condition, were exposed to the weather for the duration of the crossing, resulting in frequent attacks of illness and deaths even on these short voyages. Rather than signaling a symbolic new beginning, docking and debarkation at the Liverpool waterfront delivered the already fragile and frightened emigrants into a gauntlet that threatened their plans, their few possessions, and their physical safety.

Off-loaded and queued up like so much livestock on the dock, the Irish refugees fell immediately under the scrutiny of the local authorities and of thieves and con-men. Liverpool, a city of some three hundred thousand in the mid-1800s, was experiencing the landing of an equal number of Irish on an annual basis during the Famine years. Estimates of the time classified some thirty to forty percent of those Irish as "paupers" without the intention or means to continue on to a trans-Atlantic relocation. The local police literally scanned the Irish as the throngs exited ships in an attempt to spot the sick or destitute who could, under the laws of the day, be brought in front of a magistrate and immediately returned across the Irish Sea to the homeland they had fled.

The risk of police detention, however, paled in comparison to the victimization of the Irish emigrants by Liverpool's underworld predators, who staked out the docks for the express purpose of swindling the ragged Irish out of whatever few possessions or money they had left. The fleecing schemes ran the gamut from stolen luggage, price gouging, counterfeit monetary exchange, and ship ticket frauds. Runners and brokers, promising to help the disoriented Irish, colluded with innkeepers and boardinghouse owners to hustle the emigrants who needed temporary rooms while they waited for their trans-Atlantic ship departure date to arrive. Sadly, these successful swindles resulted in emigrants losing the means to continue their journey, forcing them back to Ireland or trapping them in the slums of Liverpool as they sought work to survive. Even more sadly, some earlier Irish emigrants who had arrived and stayed in Liverpool joined the locals in these criminal enterprises and lured their trusting fellow countrymen into the very hands of those who victimized them. For the Flannellys and thousands of other fugitive families like them, leaving Liverpool for America would prove no less difficult than getting there in the first place.

Whether by perceptive planning, the fingerings of fate, or the grace of God, our Flannellys were among those who emerged from the labyrinth that was Liverpool to board the ship that was to take them to America. But, before their feet would next step on dry land, they would have to survive another test of endurance in yet another alien and risk-laden environment, that of a four- to six-week journey at sea as steerage class passengers.

CHAPTER 8

Farewell, farewell and what is more, Receive my blessing from this shore

So goes the first of two couplets from a nineteenth-century engraving depicting Mother Erin in the guise of a beautiful dark-haired woman in a classical emerald green gown watching emigrant ships departing an Irish port. Ironically, Irish emigrants bound for North America out of Liverpool would get one last chance to see their homeland as their ships skirted the coast of Ireland and made their way to the open seas, undoubtedly a bittersweet moment for them. Some of them mistook the Irish shoreline for America. Author Herman Melville, who spent time working as a seaman including a trans-Atlantic voyage in the company of poor Irish famine emigrants, described it in his book *Redburn:_*

> "They were the most simple people I had ever seen. They seemed to have no adequate idea of distances; and, to them, America must have seemed as a place just over a river. Every morning some of them came on deck, to see how much nearer we were: and one old man would stand for hours together, looking straight off the bows, as if he expected to see New York every

minute, when, perhaps, we were yet two thousand miles distant, and steering, moreover, against a headwind."

Our Flannellys bought passage to America on the packet ship *Marmion*, named for the Sir Walter Scott epic poem of the same name. The *Marmion* sailed for Robert L. Taylor and Nathaniel W. Merrill's line (known in Liverpool as the Black Star Line), an American shipping concern based in New York. The *Marmion* was built in 1846 by William Webb's well-regarded firm. She was a wooden sailing ship of nine hundred tons with two decks and was about one hundred seventy feet long and thirty-five feet wide. The Flannellys, by whatever rationale employed, seem to have made one of the better choices of available ships, as the *Marmion* was only in service for about eight months, having made only two trans-Atlantic crossings (and back) in that period and, being an American registered ship, was subject to the United States' more stringent passenger regulations. That is not to say it was an easy trip, just that passage on a relatively new American-flagged ship should have been a damn sight better than passage on an older British registered ship, not to mention the worst of those: the aptly named "coffin ships" often hired by landlords for the "assisted emigration" of their tenants. Notorious for their poor condition (to the point of non-seaworthiness), propensity for the poorest sanitary conditions, and rampant incubation of in-voyage diseases like the dreaded "ship fever" (typhus) and death, the name "coffin ship" was duly earned at the expense of thousands of the most vulnerable of Irish emigrants.

The Flannellys were, as would be expected, "steerage" class passengers on the *Marmion*. In total, the *Marmion* had about three hundred passengers, the majority in steerage and the majority of those Irish emigrants, the others on board being predominantly Germans. Who were those Irish in steerage? Let me tell you about them. They were one hundred eighty-six (to be exact) men, women, and children. One hundred twelve were adults (eighteen or older), exactly half men and half women, fifty-six of each gender. The oldest woman was fifty (assuming each told the truth about her age) and the oldest man was sixty (likewise). There were seventy-four youngsters from the age of one to seventeen years, fifty-two of them twelve years old or younger, and twenty-two between thirteen and seventeen years old. There were many more families than people traveling alone. There were forty families of three or more people and among those, fifteen families of six or more traveling together. Our Flannellys, a family of eight, were among the largest families in steerage and only a family of nine, the Dugans, was larger. Steerage on that voyage was a veritable Irish townland on water. Among the hundred eighty-six Irish in steerage were McCaffreys (eight of them), McCanns, McCabes, McGuires, Naughtons (eight of them as well), Kelleys, Duffys, Reillys, Stewarts, Healys, Daleys, McGraths, Bradys (eight of them too), Colemans, O'Neils, Monoghans, Harleys, Terrells, Connells, Collinses, Kilroys, Feeneys, Murphys, McFaddens, Muldoons, Callaghans, Quinns, Conlins, McElroys, Rooneys, McCues, Cosgroves, Byrons, Gardiners, Tyes, and Donnellys. Odds are that among the few personal possessions these humble clans carried on-board was a favorite tin whistle or a much-loved old fiddle played to pass the time, soothe fragile souls, and rekindle once-lively spirits as the days, weeks, and miles slowly came and went.

The Irish in steerage would have been "between decks" as the term is used: a deck over them (the main deck) and a deck under their feet. The cargo hold would have been below the main deck as well. Passengers were allotted a very narrow, confined bunk space and men and women bunked in mixed company with little or no privacy. Chamber pots (or slop buckets) were used for relieving oneself. Access down to the steerage compartment was via ladders at the fore and main hatches. If those hatches were open, some ventilation was provided. In the event of weather issues or high seas, the hatches would be closed and steerage passengers remained confined in the belly of the ship until conditions improved and the hatches were reopened. The only light came from a few hanging lamps that threw off a dim glow. Steerage passengers were kept segregated from first- and second-class passengers and were often treated harshly by the ship's crew. They were permitted to "get air" on the main deck and some cooking could usually be done up top as well subject to the long line of those waiting for a chance to do so. Steerage passengers were primarily responsible for providing their own provisions of food as the ship company only supplied the most basic of food and water. Having little or no experience traveling by ship, seasickness and retching would have been commonplace and even under the best circumstances, such close quarters meant illness and disease spread quickly, only making conditions more unpleasant and dangerous. What were they thinking night after night as they lay on their eighteen-inch-wide bunk listening to the wind and waves slapping the sails and ribs of the ship, trying to close their eyes and retreat into sleep to escape the smells, coughing, and crying around them, not to mention their own fears and apprehension? So it would be for at least four weeks and over three thousand miles, traveling in the November cold and winter gales of the Atlantic seas.

CHAPTER **9**

None but the Frugal, Industrious, and Temperate

The seemingly endless journey did come to an end when the *Marmion* came into the East River in late November 1846 and docked at South Street in Manhattan among dozens of ships sailing for the competing lines of the day, including Black Star, Black Ball, and many others. The population of New York City was about a half million. By the time the Statue of Liberty would be completed in 1886, the population would triple as the result of welcoming immigrants from all over the world for the prior four decades.

The Flannellys arrived nine years before Castle Garden in Lower Manhattan became a formal immigration processing facility. At the time of their arrival in 1846, the Customs House in Manhattan was responsible for the review of immigrant passengers on incoming ships. After that, immigrants like the Flannellys were set loose on the bustling docks of New York City. Imagine their wide eyes as they picked up their few bags or trunks and tentatively made their first steps away from the ship where they spent weeks of cramped confinement with two hundred fellow steerage passengers, venturing out into the streets of a huge city to find a small space to call their own. No doubt Irish speakers, their ears would have been assaulted by talk all around them in a language they likely did not comprehend. And then there were the "runners" who frequented the docks on behalf of disreputable boardinghouse owners who specialized in victimizing newly arrived immigrants. In their publication of 1845 directed to potential Irish emigrants, The Irish Emigrant Society of New York counseled as follows:

> "In New York, the emigrant must be aware of certain boarding-houses established here for his special accommodation; but which too often, prove to be dens where he can be cheated, plundered and insulted. He can avoid all this by either consulting with one of the agents of the Irish Emigrant Society, who is generally at the quarantine clock where the emigrants are first landed, or when he comes up to the city, by applying without delay at the office of the society. Before going to any boarding house he should make a distinct bargain with the keeper of it for his board, having expressly understood whether he is to settle by the day or by the week, whether he is at liberty to leave at any time, and pay to the time of leaving, or is to be held responsible for a certain period, whether he stops so long or not, etc. In fact he cannot be too careful in his dealings with the boarder house keepers, or too particular in the bargain he makes with them; and by having a fellow passenger present at the time witness to the bargain, he will in many instances save himself much trouble, vexation and expense."

The publication went on to give the following general admonishment to the Irish aspiring to become Americans:

> "None but the frugal, the industrious, and the temperate, can hope for success in America. Such indeed may emigrate with confident expectation of a prosperous result. They must be prepared, however, to encounter disappointments, to surmount difficul-

ties and not to be overcome by apparent discourage-
ment..."

Unlike so many Irish immigrants of the day, our Flannellys
did not settle in New York City and instead made their way to the
quaint suburb of Jersey City, across the Hudson River from New
York. Jersey City was in its early years as a municipality when
the Flannellys arrived, having only come into existence in 1804
under the auspices of The Associates of the Jersey Company and
its leadership, including two former New York City mayors and
a New York attorney. It was not until 1820 that the Associates
petitioned for an official municipal charter and it was not until
1838 that Jersey City was officially made separate from the Town
of Bergen. Just eight years later, the Flannellys arrived in America
and then Jersey City, a bucolic community of some six thousand
residents, most of them American-born Protestants of the middle
and upper classes. This Jersey City had its roots in early Dutch set-
tlers and their descendants, as did New York City. In the first half
of the nineteenth century, New York steadily grew as a population
and commerce center with Jersey City orbiting it like a small moon
and becoming a preferred place of residence for professionals
and elite working in New York who could hop a ferry to New York
for a roundtrip fare of twenty-five cents.

The Jersey City of the 1840s was home to farms but not yet
to industry or manufacturing, making it something of a "bedroom
community" of its day, not unlike suburban enclaves of today that
are within commutable distances of large cities drawing thousands
for employment. I can't say how the Flannellys made the decision
to make Jersey City their home except to speculate that either they
had Irish connections of family or friends there or, looking for
some sense of the countryside they had known in Ireland while still
having proximity to New York, they were drawn there, the former
being more likely.

Less than four years after the Flannellys stepped off the Mar-

mion and began a new life in America, they are found in the 1850 US census for Jersey City. The data reveal that our Flannellys were among about sixty-nine hundred Jersey City residents captured in the census-taking in August 1850 that recorded about thirty-two hundred white males, thirty-five hundred white females, sixty-nine "colored" males, and seventy-three "colored" females. The census-takers visited seven hundred twenty-five dwellings with a total of nearly thirteen hundred households. Imagine only seven hundred twenty-five dwellings in Jersey City! The Flannellys were one of three families, all Irish-born, in their dwelling, which was number seven hundred one of the total seven hundred twenty-five visited. None of those three families were owners of the dwelling. Of the twenty-two people living in "701," twenty-one were born in Ireland, ages ranging from one to forty-seven, and twelve were children. In fact, the only American-born resident at "701" was MaryAnn Flannelly, then William and Mary's youngest child born in Jersey City in 1848/49, two years after their arrival in America. Within eighteen months after the census was taken, William and Mary would have their last child, son William.

Looking closer at the overall census data, I counted about seventeen hundred fifty residents who identified their place of birth as "Ireland," making them about twenty-five percent of the total population. About four hundred eighty of the enumerated households were recorded with an Irish-born person as the head of household. Presumptively, that would equate to about thirty-eight percent of the total recorded households. Comparably, about five hundred households, or thirty-nine percent, were recorded with an American-born person as the head of household. The remaining three hundred or so households, or about twenty-three percent, were recorded with a non-American, non-Irish person at the head of the household, the majority indicating their birthplace as England, Scotland, or Germany, along with a sprinkling of others, including Canada, France, and even one each of Cuba, Sweden, Mexico, and Switzerland.

Of the twenty-four dwellings preceding the Flannellys' residence in the census record, thirteen were inhabited by single families; twenty-six other households cohabited in the remaining eleven dwellings. Of the final twenty-four dwellings following the Flannellys' residence in the census record, only one dwelling was inhabited by a single household; the other fifty-eight households cohabited in twenty-three dwellings. Those statistics reflect the fact that most dwellings were home to two or three households. Those not living in multi-family dwellings included a German tobacconist, a French merchant, an English railroad car builder, a native-born block and pump maker's family that listed about fourteen thousand dollars in real estate owned value, a native-born Navy lieutenant listing four thousand two hundred dollars in real estate owned value, an Irish iron founder, an Irish glassmaker, an Irish laborer with fourteen hundred dollars in real estate owned, an Irish teamster with thirteen hundred dollars in real estate owned, an Irish stonecutter with nine thousand two hundred dollars in real estate owned, and an Irish grocer with six thousand dollars in real estate owned.

William Flannelly, like the majority of his fellow Irish-born residents, was listed with the occupation "laborer," although there were a few Irish-born tradesmen such as glassblowers, potters, shoemakers, wheelwrights, stonecutters, tailors, and carpenters in the census. The professionals and businessmen (doctors, lawyers, glass manufacturers, merchants, bookkeepers, editors, customs house clerks, grocers, life insurance agents, railroad agents, engineers, ferry masters/captains, tax collectors, jewelers, sea captains, ship owners, printers, architects, druggists, etc.) were almost exclusively American-born men. The census entries also indicate that William and Mary Flannelly were unable to read and write but show that their three youngest sons, John, Patrick, and Edward (all under ten years old), had attended school during 1850. Within a year after this 1850 census-taking, neighboring Van Vorst Township would be merged into Jersey City, adding over six hundred dwellings and more than nine hundred families and instantly increasing the population of the city by some sixty-five percent to over eleven thousand and the number of dwellings by over eighty percent as well.

The Jersey City directory for 1849-50 includes a listing for William Flannelly ("Flanley"), laborer, living at 4 Morgan's Row, Jersey City. This is the earliest address found for our Flannellys. The Jersey City directories for 1850-51 and 1851-52 have a listing for William Flannelly ("Flanley"), laborer, living at 3 Morgan's Row (near Greene St.), Jersey City. The next directory, for 1852-53, lists William Flannelly (also spelled "Flanley"), laborer, living at the corner of Washington and Steuben streets. The directory of 1853-54 lists William at that same address. The next directory (1854-55) shows William, laborer, at 3 Morgan's Row, near Washington Street.

The directories for 1855-61 list William at 251 South Third Street. The directory for 1862-63 does not include William but does have a listing for his son Owen, marble cutter, at the 251 South Third address. The 1860 census records the full Flannelly family: William and Mary and their eight children aged seven to twenty-five, all in the household. Abby, twenty-five, would marry the following year. Michael, twenty, is a laborer. Owen, twenty-two, and your grandfather John, seventeen, are shown as marble-cutters. Patrick, fourteen, Edward, twelve, MaryAnn, ten, and William, seven, are all shown attending school. They are living in a dwelling with one other household, the Patrick McKenna family. Patrick McKenna is an Irish-born carpenter and likely a widower as he is living just with his seven children, all born in New Jersey.

That census tells a surprising story about the Flannellys' and McKennas' neighbors in 1860. Taking the forty closest dwellings, the twenty preceding and the twenty following the Flannellys in that census, the Flannellys and the McKennas are the only families with an Irish-born head of household. There are a few German-born and English-born heads of household but the overwhelming majority of the families are headed by American-born men with listed professions including lawyer, civil engineer (three), merchant (ten), pencil case maker, cigar maker (two), tailor (three), railroad conductor, lumber merchant, printer, engraver, grocer, bookbinder, ink maker, teacher, accountant, pilot, watchmaker (two), shoemaker, freight agent, ship chandler, miller, and jeweler. Thirty of the forty dwellings are occupied by only one household and ten are occupied by two households headed by non-Irish men. And then there is the dwelling where the Flannellys and McKennas lived, an Irish island in a sea of native-born professionals, merchants, and tradesmen!

CHAPTER 10

Community and Catholicism

Before there was "Jersey City," there was a marshy, sandy ferry landing known as Paulus Hook serving the village of Bergen. The ferry carried people across the Hudson to Manhattan, less than a mile's distance. The Associates of the Jersey Company's land lease included rights to the ferry. In the first decade of the nineteenth century, the Associates laid out a street plan for their new village showing thirteen hundred forty-four lots, many of them literally "in the water." For a variety of reasons, including a title dispute with the City of New York and economic problems, the lots didn't sell and the planned village did not materialize. Instead, Paulus Hook attracted an unwelcome cast of characters, including thieves, gamblers, and drifters. Over time, travelers and transients, including itinerant laborers, and some workers associated with a local distillery, tobacco factory, and glassworks came and went and businesses grew up around them: hotels, a couple dozen saloons and betting venues. The Associates had envisioned a positive "spillover" effect from New York City that would lead to a growing village of quality families leaving the City for greener pastures. On the contrary, the new village had more of a Wild West flavor.

In an effort to get control and stabilize the village, the Associates instituted law enforcement and began trying to attract

(Protestant) churches. About a decade after The Associates of the Jersey Company succeeded in getting a municipal charter, the Company donated marshland on Grand Street to be used by the new Catholic parish of St. Peter for its first church building. Up until that time and while St. Peter's was under construction, Jersey City's Catholics (estimated to be about one hundred souls) would have had to travel across the Hudson River to Manhattan to attend mass at St. Peter's on Barclay Street or St. Patrick's on Mott Street. Sometimes, priests from New York City rowed across the Hudson to Jersey City and celebrated mass in Catholic homes or circuit-riding priests did likewise.

Church construction began in 1831 with Catholic volunteers from Jersey City and New York working for the next four years with picks and spades to fill in the lots with sand so the property would be buildable. Despite all those efforts, a piling failure caused the building to collapse before completion. Construction was restarted and services began to be held at the new church in 1837, nine years before the Flannellys arrived from Ireland. One of their fellow County Sligo immigrants who arrived in America in 1836, a Patrick Rooney, plastered the church walls and later started the first Sunday school for Catholic children even before St. Peter's was completed. He and others recalled that, in response to the collapse, non-Catholics came forward with assistance and support.

In 1844, Irish-born Father John Kelly, once a missionary priest in Africa, was appointed pastor of St. Peter's five hundred Catholics, a job he embraced with that same missionary spirit and fervor. St. Peter's parochial school, believed to be the first Catholic school in New Jersey, had been started in about 1836 in the basement of a residential home. About the time that Father Kelly came to St. Peter's, the parish school relocated to the church basement. In the early 1850s the first of two orders of religious Sisters helped staff the school. This was surely the school attended by the three young Flannelly boys and later by their younger American-born siblings, William and MaryAnn, in the late 1850s and early 1860s.

In 1839, the trustees of St. Peter's parish had petitioned the governing council of the City requesting an appropriation in support of the parish school based on seemingly similar support given over the preceding years to schools associated with local Protestant churches. The request from St. Peter's was denied. Another request was submitted in 1842 and would have been granted if St. Peter's agreed to turn over its school to the local government, which, understandably, was not acceptable. In 1846, just months before the Flannellys arrived in Jersey City and joined the parish, St. Peter's, led by Father Kelly, once again petitioned the city authorities for school funding at a time when Jersey City's public schools were severely overcrowded and a new school act opened the door more broadly to denominational school support. Although those factors and Father Kelly's resolve seemed destined for success, after months and years of tension and political struggle, St. Peter's was once again denied and left to its own devices while comparable Protestant-associated schools were deemed eligible for aid.

By 1863 Father Kelly, seeing the steady growth of the parishioner numbers, acquired additional land on Grand Street, and work on a new, larger church began in 1865. Father Kelly, an outspoken advocate for the Catholic minority in Jersey City, would not live to see the new church completed. He died in April, 1866 after a twenty-year tenure that saw dynamic growth and laid a firm foundation for the future of the parish to which he was so devoted.

Father Kelly's legacy would grow large from the modest seeds he planted for his Catholic flock. In his *History of Jersey City*, published in 1895, Alexander McLean included a subsection titled "Roman Catholic Schools," stating that the enrollment in that year had reached about seven thousand four hundred sixty-three students (more than the total of all Jersey City residents in 1850) taught by one hundred twenty-five teachers. In another chapter McLean covers the history of the churches in Jersey City. From one fledgling parish, St. Peter's, and not in small part as the result of Father Kelly's tireless efforts to serve the needs of Catholics in Jersey City and surrounding towns, five new parish churches grew from missions of St. Peter's to self-sufficiency as St. Bridget's, St. Michael's, St. Mary's, St. Patrick's, and St. Joseph's from the 1850s to the 1870s. Our own Irish family celebrated marriages and baptisms and buried their dead from St. Peter's, St. Michael's, St. Patrick's, and St. Bridget's during the nineteenth century (and you, Kate, were married in the St. Joseph's rectory in 1921). Seventeen of our early Flannellys are interred in contiguous plots in St. Peter's Cemetery, those gravesites purchased by William Flannelly in 1864.

The Jersey City Catholic minority of barely one hundred in about 1830 would grow over the following decades, reaching over seventeen hundred or twenty-five percent of the population at the time of the 1850 US census. Notwithstanding the size of that population increase or the sizable percentage it represented, Irish Catholics had not made comparable progress integrating their own into the existing political or social structure in Jersey City, that continuing to be the province of native-born non-Catholics. The conventional wisdom was that Irish immigrant residents, who steadfastly resisted attempts to coerce them to renounce their Catholic faith and embrace the "established" Protestant church, were stubborn, wrong-headed, and being led astray by their clergy. Their "popish" beliefs and growing numbers were believed to present a threat to the native-borns' control of politics and societal authority. These fears of loss of position and control and so economic superiority are the same ones that have attached themselves to each successive wave of immigrants, causing distrust, animosity, and even violence. An 1883 article in *The New York Times* reported on seven hundred sixty Irish immigrants whose passage was paid by the British government in their latest effort to shed segments of the Irish population. Having recently arrived at the Castle Garden immigration station, they were described in very favorable terms by the officials at Castle Garden, who characterized them as "industrious and thrifty people" who "speak English well" and "will not become burdens in any way." To put a fine point on it, the Castle Garden superintendent, Mr. Jackson, stated that he considered these Irish immigrants "very much better than the Italians who come to America." So it is that bottom-rung immigrants are propelled up the social ladder as new ethnic immigrant groups knock at America's front door.

In the United States at large during the mid-nineteenth century, native-born men formed political groups such as the "Know Nothing Party," dedicated to the "protection" of native-born society from the perceived negative effects of the growing population of Irish and other immigrants. These sentiments and movements and the resulting active discrimination against the Irish and other immigrant groups persisted through the period of the Civil War and beyond and successfully held back the progress of Irish immigrant political enfranchisement in Jersey City for many years despite the growing numbers of Irish voters. Gerrymandering of election districts and the rewriting of laws for the specific purpose of thwarting Irish candidates in Jersey City were commonplace.

In 1860, Jersey City had a four-ward structure and the Irish residents were slowly learning to join together to participate in and influence local politics and government, including the police force. Their votes were actively courted, particularly by the Democrats, but they were not part of the Democratic Party leadership, which stayed in the hands of native-born men. Although inroads were being made by the new Irish-Americans, anti-Catholic sentiment remained prevalent through the decade of the 1860s. Redrawing of wards and districts in the city were common as a means of segmenting majority Irish neighborhoods and so diluting the effects of the Irish vote. Just the same, in 1867 the first Irish mayoral candidate was on the ballot, although he was defeated by a local businessman and former Know-Nothing Party member.

The 1860 US census recorded a little over twenty-nine thousand Jersey City residents. The census showed that non-native-born males equated to about sixty percent of the total adult male population, Irish males representing the overwhelming majority of that sixty percent. Those Irish men, mostly Catholic, were largely unskilled laborers working in factories and for the railroad and they were poor, living in tenements and shanties. Conversely, the native-born adult males residing in Jersey City, mostly Protestant, represented the skilled and businessmen and, as such, those of economic advantage.

Ultimately, by the 1870s, the growing tide of Irish residents, whose community leaders had learned how to play the political game from their native-born "betters," could not be held back any longer as they formed beneficial political alliances and assumed various roles in Jersey City government. Irish immigrants continued to come to Jersey City in large numbers, assimilating into the fabric of their city and seeing it become home to a major railroad hub, industrialization, and manufacturing during the second half of the nineteenth century. By 1890, the population of Jersey City was over one hundred fifty thousand!

CHAPTER **11**

The Jersey Blues

About fifteen years after the Flannellys settled in Jersey City, the US Civil War broke out and President Abraham Lincoln called for troops to be raised to put down the secessionist rebellion of the Confederacy. This was in early 1861. As an enticement to enlistees, the federal government offered cash sign-on bonuses known as "bounties," payable at the end of the enlistment period. These incentives ranged as high as one hundred dollars or more, a small fortune for many who joined the Union Army as a result. Over four hundred thousand immigrants are said to have enlisted in the Union Army. Others also joined the Confederacy in smaller numbers. Of those numbers, one hundred seventy thousand were Irish immigrants. As the war went on, quota systems were put in place to raise needed additional Union troops, including in Hudson County communities. A piece in *The New York Times* in July 1863 reported that the Governor of New Jersey had issued a proclamation indicating recruit quotas needed to fill the ranks of New Jersey's regiments. The Hudson County quota was six hundred twenty-three men. Jersey City's share of that quota was forty-eight from the First Ward, sixty-seven from the Second Ward, forty-eight from the Third Ward, sixty-seven from the Fourth Ward, fifty-three from the Fifth Ward, and twenty-seven from the Sixth Ward, a total of three hundred ten of the overall Hudson County quota. For those who had the means, military service could be avoided by paying another man to serve for them.

Two of William and Mary Flannelly's six sons were among those Irish immigrant enlistees. Owen Flannelly joined the 2nd Regiment, Company G of the New Jersey Foot Militia Infantry in April, 1861 for a short three-month commitment, the expectation of the federal government being that the Southern rebellion would be over in a matter of months. He would have reported to Trenton on May 1, 1861 and the regiment then left for Washington, DC and remained there into June attached to General Runyon's forces defending the US Capitol. The regiment participated in the occupation of Arlington Heights, Virginia and in the construction of Fort Runyon before advancing on Manassas, Virginia in mid-July for the Battle of Bull Run, where his regiment was a "reserve unit." The battle at Bull Run was the opening battle of the Civil War, and the Union troops, inexperienced and ill-prepared, suffered an embarrassing defeat when Union soldiers broke ranks in a helter-skelter retreat. Owen was mustered out in Trenton in late July, 1861 at the expiration of his ninety-day term and did not re-enlist.

Your grandfather, Owen's brother John J. Flannelly, enlisted for a three-year term at the local Jersey City recruiting office on August 9, 1861 for a promised hundred-dollar bounty payment. He was to join the 6th New Jersey Volunteer Infantry, Company C, formed under a July 1861 Act of Congress. Our John, just nineteen at the time he enlisted, was about to start an odyssey that would take him four hundred miles from home to Tidewater Virginia, where he would soon be struggling through mud-soaked battlefields in relentless rain, fighting to survive hand-to-hand combat with other American boys and men.

John reported to his unit during the week of August 19th, most likely going to the old church on Grand Street in Jersey City, a designated mustering point for new recruits. From there, he and the others in his company would have marched to the

Pennsylvania Railroad Depot, where a special train would take them on the three-hour trip to Trenton. According to an account of a private (Alfred Bellard) in the New Jersey 5th Regiment who joined the Union Army in Jersey City on the very same day as our John, departing soldier trains in Jersey City were sent off to the cheers and tears of well-wishing and worried friends and relatives of the departing recruits. Bellard's regiment served side-by-side with John Flannelly's unit and so his detailed chronicles of daily life in the New Jersey Volunteers give us the gift of really knowing and feeling what John experienced straight from the pen of another young Hudson County soldier, also an immigrant to the United States.

Bellard described what he characterized as an "artificial examination" upon arrival in Trenton, where the recruits queued up in a line, called out by name one by one to attest to their own good health, got "thumped on the chest" by a doctor, and "pronounced in good condition." That was followed by a swearing-in and oath and a march to Camp Olden on the outer edge of Trenton, where they were assigned to a campground and had to pitch tents where they would sleep. A blanket, knapsack, tin cup, plate, and utensils were supplied to each man and, of course, the blue Union uniform.

The New Jersey 6th Regiment, including thirty-eight officers and eight hundred sixty privates and non-commissioned men, left New Jersey on September 10, 1861. They would have traveled by train, most likely to Camden, then crossing the Delaware River by ferry to Philadelphia. Then it would have been another train trip to Maryland, probably stopping at Havre de Grace and Baltimore and then on to Washington, DC, where the 6th was attached to the Army of the Potomac under General George B. McClellan along with its New Jersey sister units, the 5th, 7th and 8th regiments, and forming the twenty-six hundred men of the 2nd New Jersey Brigade known as the "Jersey Blues." The 6th made an expedition to Lower Maryland in early November 1861 and camped on Meridian Hill

(Washington) in December 1861 and at Budd's Ferry into April 1862 under General Joseph Hooker's command.

Also in the New Jersey 6th Regiment were brothers Samuel and Edward Fox from Trenton. The Fox brothers wrote home to their other brothers, George and Charles, all four having been orphaned about five years earlier. Their surviving letters are plain language narratives that reach out to us across a century and a half and, like Alfred Bellard's more expansive chronicles, give context, color, and reality to what John (and Owen) Flannelly lived and survived, the routines of daily life, and the raw, scarring experiences of the violence of war. At Camp Meridian in late 1861, Edward Fox described meeting a slave left behind in his owner's deserted house and how that slave generously gave him writing paper, which he used to write home. Not long after, Samuel described moving to Budd's Point and talked about walking thirteen miles wading through mud up to their knees and waist-high water. The brothers thanked the folks at home for sending newspapers such as *Frank Leslie's Pictorial* and told them to look out for money they had sent home, some for the needs of their youngest brother and the rest to be saved for their return home.

The 2nd New Jersey Brigade would be part of the Peninsula Campaign, McClellan's strategic plan to take Richmond, Virginia from the Confederates by coming up from Yorktown. The Fox brothers, Alfred Bellard, and our John Flannelly and their New Jersey comrades in arms were boarded onto boats for the trip down the Potomac River to Fortress Monroe, an impressive fortification on the eastern end of the Peninsula. By the first week of May, more than one hundred thousand Union soldiers were mustered there.

Among the sights, sounds, and happenings that must have left our boys wide-eyed as they prepared for their first real encounter with the Confederates were naval skirmishes between the Confederate iron-clad *Virginia* (originally known as the *Merrimack* when in the control of the Union Navy) and the stranger-looking

Monitor, the Union iron-clad. Alfred Bellard described "swarms" of ships at Fort Monroe, including gunboats, tugs, steam frigates, and ocean and river steamers. He sized the *Monitor* up as a "cheese box on a raft"! Despite all that, the Union Navy and the *Monitor* were unsuccessful in their efforts to disable or capture the *Virginia*. That ultimately meant a failure to gain control of the James and York rivers, which in turn meant that the Union troops would have to move from Yorktown toward Richmond overland, fighting their way up the Peninsula, pushing back Confederate forces all the way.

Confederate forces had been busy digging in around Yorktown, building a line of defenses and maneuvering troops to successfully create the impression (to the leadership of the Union forces) that their numbers were significantly higher than they actually were. And then in April, as the Union's General McClellan was preparing to muster troops at Fort Monroe and begin the drive up the Peninsula, the weather turned against him as spring rains began their relentless battering, washing out roads and leaving behind rivers of mud, muck, and mire that would bog down the movement of equipment and men while creating a breeding ground for diseases like malaria and cholera that would strike down dozens of his soldiers.

In his daily journal, Alfred Bellard described getting orders to move on the 21st of April, 1862, saying that "it had been raining all day and the roads were simply horrible" making progress "slow and tedious" as they passed the Confederate earthwork defenses, which they could not see until they were nearly on top of them. When they made camp that evening, the rain came on again, flooding the ground with several inches of water, soaking blankets and other supplies. In the darkness, rain, and mud, Bellard and some others were sent out to dig trenches with picks and spades. More misery. As the days went by and the month of May approached, the troops worked day and night building fortifications and trenches as the two sides exchanged fire and shellings went back and forth. The New Jersey 6th Regiment, John Flannelly's unit, came in from picket duty with two men wounded by a Confederate shelling. Soldiers on both sides were literally dug into flooded, mud-filled trenches and sickness was rampant. This was the Siege of Yorktown, which ended when the Confederate forces quietly evacuated their earthwork defenses after delaying the forward progress of the Union troops.

The Confederates had fallen back and then created another line of defense midway up the Peninsula, which gave McClellan and the Union forces safe use of the James River for naval support and transport of additional Union troops to join McClellan. Those Confederate defenses, however, included the heavily fortified, imposing Fort MacGruder near the historic former capital city of Williamsburg. There were multiple huge defensive earthworks comprising the fort and its surrounds. Alfred Bellard wrote about "infernal machines," which he called torpedoes, planted in the road to Williamsburg by the Confederates. These mines were triggered by a stick or branch planted near them and killed several of Bellard's fellow soldiers as they moved up the Peninsula.

On May 5, 1862 as the cold, driving rain continued, Union troops, soaked and muddy, approached Williamsburg and Fort MacGruder. In the book *New Jersey and The Rebellion*, authored by John Y. Foster and published in 1868, the march to Williamsburg was described as follows:

> "The Jersey Brigade, leaving Yorktown at two o'clock, pushed forward with all possible rapidity until eleven o'clock, when it bivouacked in a swamp some five miles from Williamsburg. The night was intensely dark and rainy, the roads were muddy and difficult, and the men were sorely exhausted by labor in the trenches and want of sleep; but notwithstanding all obstacles and discouragements the troops pressed eagerly forward, all anxious to participate in the struggle which was felt to be

imminent. The position of the enemy, as described in General Hooker's report, was one of great strength. The main work, Fort MacGruder, occupied the centre, at the junction of the Yorktown and Hampton roads, with a cordon of redoubts on either side, extending as far as the eye could reach. For a distance of half a mile in front of these works, the forest had been felled to obstruct the advance of our infantry, while a belt of clear open land, six hundred or seven hundred yards in width, dotted all over with rifle pits, stretched between the tangled abbatis and the fort and redoubts. In the immediate front of the redoubts, the plain was furrowed by winding ravines, which were swept by the guns of the enemy."

Foster went on to describe the scene where the men of the 5th, 6th, 7th, and 8th New Jersey regiments, including young John Flannelly, were fighting:

"At this time the rain was falling in torrents and the men stood half-leg deep in mire and water. Steadily advancing through the underbrush, the gallant regiments soon came upon the enemy's forces, and at once opened a vigorous fire. Here, for three hours, the conflict raged with desperate fury. Commanding the ground at every point, the fire of the enemy was pitilessly destructive, and did not slacken for a moment. But the brave fellows into whose faces it was poured, stood firmly and unflinchingly, sometimes, indeed, pushed back a little space, but as surely hurling the rebels, bleeding and shattered, back to their works."

Bellard painted a picture of the first sight of the Fort: "rebels" entrenched near the fort, sharpshooters in rifle pits, and felled tree fortifications of eight to ten feet high in places. The Jersey Blues made their way through those downed trees and John Flannelly's 6th New Jersey regiment took up a forward position at a nearby ravine that would be the site of some ten thousand troops locked in brutal fighting for more than four hours on the morning of May 5, 1862. As the battle raged on, lines broke down, men were separated and fought alone or in small groups, visibility severely reduced due to rain and smoke.

In his memoir, *Gone for a Soldier*, edited by David Herbert Donald and published in 1975 more than a century after he penned the words, Bellard goes on:

> "Fighting soon became general, and the wounded were sent to the rear, while the dead lay where they fell. Shot, shell and bullets were now flying round lively, and it was about as dangerous to be in the woods on account of the falling trees and limbs that were cut off by the shells, as it was in the front.

> "Dead men were laying in all directions. In walking over the field, some would be seen with their legs or arms shot off, others with the top or side the head cut off as with a knife (which in this case was a piece of shell)... In a ravine that was so ably defended by the rest of our brigade, the dead rebels were piled one on the other... Our division went into camp...and the sad task of burying the dead commenced, the 8th New Jersey having lost the most. A large trench about 100 feet long and about 8 feet in width and 18 inches deep was dug and into this wholesale grave about 80 men were placed side by side, with their uniforms on and the earth being covered over them... Our Regiment (New Jersey 5th) lost in the Battle of Williamsburg about 103 in killed, wounded and missing."

Edward Fox, part of John Flannelly's New Jersey 6th Regiment, wrote home to his brother days after the Battle of Williamsburg:

"Hurrah for the Gallant 5th, 6th, 7th and 8th New Jersey Volunteers...the Jersey Boys done all the fighting and got no praise for it...we was first in the fight and the last ones out...our brigade and Hauckers (Hooker's) division were fighting the main fort (Fort MacGruder) and forse (force) of the rebles (rebels) and they numbered about sixty thousand and we were in mud up to our knees and only had two Batteries of Artelry (Artillery) and the horses had to die in the mud and just to think of our two Brigades keeping back sixty thousand rebles (rebels)...it was a horrible sight to see the poor fellows killed and wounded some with their legs off and arms off and heds (heads) blowed off..."

The Confederates once again evacuated their defensive positions after stalling the Union troops' progress up the Peninsula, and moved back toward Richmond to consolidate with other forces preparing to defend the Confederate capital against capture by the Union troops. The Union forces then occupied Williamsburg as the town was flooded with wounded soldiers from both sides. The 1860 census for Williamsburg recorded seven hundred forty-two whites, one hundred twenty-one free blacks, and seven hundred forty-three black slaves along with the two hundred seventy white and nineteen black inmates of the Eastern Lunatic Asylum of Virginia. The people of Williamsburg, aligned with the Southern cause, indignantly endured the Union occupation and post-battle chaos.

John Flannelly's Civil War military records show he was hospitalized in Williamsburg three days after the Battle of Williamsburg on May 9, 1862, but do not indicate the reason. He could very well have been one of the soldiers who lay wounded, stranded, and alone on the muddy, scarred, sulfur-choked fields around Fort MacGruder in the days following that battle. The Comte de Paris described the situation:

"Hidden under the branches of felled trees...and on the third day after the battle some were taken out who yet had a spark of life. During the evening of that same day, the dry woods were set on fire by accident; the conflagration spread rapidly, and stifling the agonized cries of those who were perhaps still waiting for the succor of their friends, swept away the last traces of the victims of the struggle."

It is also possible that he was ill, having contracted malaria as many years later he would be awarded a veteran's pension due to a variety of maladies, including "malarial poisoning," making him one of over seven thousand Civil War pensioners with that chronic condition. In early May 1992, exactly one hundred thirty years after the Battle of Williamsburg, my son, John Flannelly's great-great-great-grandson, would attend freshman orientation at the College of William and Mary in Williamsburg, one of the places used as a field hospital for soldiers after that battle, walking where his Irish immigrant ancestor had walked so many years before... unbeknownst to any of us at the time.

Military medical care during the Civil War, delivered by some ten thousand Union surgeons and about half that many Confederate counterparts, was devoid of knowledge of the essential need for sanitary conditions, and practices such as using sterile dressings and antiseptic surgical environments were unknown. At least as many men died during the Civil War from disease as from battle injuries. The diseases striking down those men included malaria, typhoid, measles, smallpox, pneumonia, tuberculosis, and the twin demons diarrhea and dysentery. Besides the natural threats of disease resulting from persistent rain and camping in swampy areas, the camps themselves were without any regulations or organization related to general sanitary practices. Amputation due to battle injuries was common and soldiers described seeing piles of limbs several feet high in field hospitals. Gangrene, sepsis, and blood poisoning stalked amputees and very large numbers died as a result.

John Flannelly's Civil War military record has an entry dated November and December 1862, which states that he is "absent" and was sent to the hospital in Williamsburg, Virginia on May 9, 1862, implying that his hospitalization had continued there. The next of the sparse entries contradicts that and indicates that for the period from October 31, 1862 (five months after his hospitalization in Williamsburg) through February 28, 1863, he was "marked as a Deserter from absent sick by order of Colonel George Burling." There is an undated entry that indicates his desertion as of January 12, 1863 and includes the address 250 South Third Street (surely a reference to 251 South Third Street, Jersey City, the home of William and Mary Flannelly and their family). The next entry, more than a year later in June 1864, states that he was arrested in May 1864 in Newark and that a thirty-dollar bounty was paid by a Captain E.M. Miller, Provost Marshal 5th Congressional District of New Jersey. Despite all those accusations and charges, the final entries in his file say he was "gained from desertion on May 28, 1864" and that the thirty-dollar bounty payment was "stopped." The Company Muster Roll was revised to show him as "present from February 29, 1864 to June 30, 1864" and indicates he was honorably mustered out in Trenton on September 7, 1864 and was to be paid nine dollars and seventy-one cents for clothing and was due the hundred-dollar bounty that no doubt was a powerful incentive for his original decision to enlist three years earlier.

Where John Flannelly went after his hospitalization in Williamsburg I cannot say nor could I discover how he put himself to rights with the Union Army authorities. Many injured soldiers became separated from their units, which moved on while those soldiers were hospitalized. Many of those injured fell in with other nearby units when released from their hospitalization. Having said that, there is no question that desertion from both the Union and Confederate ranks was a significant problem. A wide variety of causes and factors resulted in tens of thousands of men being recorded deserters or "absent without leave." Young men and boys, most away from home for the first time, found themselves utterly unprepared, lacking needed training and supplies, deprived of basic necessities for weeks at time, severely exhausted, struck down by disease, and immersed in shocking, unimaginable violence and carnage. As for the Army of the Potomac, of which John Flannelly was a member, General Hooker is said to have estimated that eighty-five thousand officers and enlisted men had deserted as of 1863. In late 1862 (the point at which John Flannelly seems to have gone missing), up to one hundred eighty thousand Union soldiers listed on muster rolls were categorized as "absent," with or without leave. To discourage desertion, threats of severe punishment were publicized and a small number of deserters were subjected to the death penalty. More often, the army let it be known that deserters who voluntarily returned would be pardoned.

The discovery of John Flannelly's service in the Union Army, participation in the bloody Battle of Williamsburg and subsequent several month stay in that historic city connected him with me, his great-great-granddaughter, like a bolt of lightning. I had been drawn to Williamsburg repeatedly over the past thirty years, first as a frequent visitor and ultimately as a part-time resident of the city for the last ten years. I had walked the streets of the historic area and the grounds of the College of William and Mary hundreds of times over those many years, never knowing our family connection. Now, those streets and my footsteps on them echo a personal past and I finally understand why I was drawn to Williamsburg time and time again. The patient, persistent whispers of time and intuition were calling me.

CHAPTER **12**

Another Bridget "Such-a-One" Journeys to America

In May 1862 as twenty-year-old Private John Flannelly lay in a Union field hospital in Williamsburg, across the Atlantic Ocean a thirteen-year-old girl named Bridget Hough (called "Delia") was preparing to leave her home and family in Ireland. By late May she would make her way to the port of Liverpool as John Flannelly and his family had done nearly sixteen years earlier and would book passage to New York in steerage class on the ship *Vanguard*. Bridget appears on the ship's passenger manifest as passenger number four hundred of the total four hundred sixteen listed. Seventy of those four hundred sixteen were cabin passengers and the other three hundred forty-six passengers were "between decks" steerage passengers traveling under the harsh, cramped conditions described earlier. The ship passenger list shows Bridget's occupation as "housemaid," making her one of seventy-five "housemaids" aged seven to sixty-two traveling on the *Vanguard*. In addition, another forty-one female passengers listed "servant" as their occupation. Together, these Irish domestics, with names like Egan, Rafferty, McIntyre, Clancy, McCabe, Murray, Hurley, Connolly, Dwyer, McCarthy, Sullivan, Bradley, Fitzsimmons, McDermott, Kelly, O'Brien, Kennelly, Casey, Boyle, and Conroy, represented one-third of the total steerage passengers. With the steady stream of Irish women coming to America with the intent of going into domestic service, they were often commonly referred to as "Bridgets." Even in 1862, a decade after the Famine years, prospects in Ireland remained bleak, particularly in rural areas, and that served as continuing incentive for Irish women to emigrate to America...even at the tender age of thirteen.

The expression "like mother, like daughter" (actually "like grandmother, like granddaughter" in this case) floats into my mind as I recognize the parallel between Delia's teenage years in domestic service and your own. Across a gulf of over forty years, family circumstances would snatch away your adolescence as cruelly as Delia's own adolescence had been taken from her, each of you instantly transformed into working "women" in service to strangers, your "betters," and each finding independence and liberation in marriage by the tender age of eighteen.

Delia Hough, born in Ireland in 1849, was the daughter of Joseph and Delia (Merryman) Hough, her mother's proper name likely being Bridget. More than that has not been discovered as of this writing but it is believed that she was a red-haired lass with freckles, those coppery tresses and fairy speckles destined to be passed on to her daughter Mary Flannelly, who passed them on to you, Kate. It appears Delia was traveling without family on the *Vanguard*, perhaps in the company of a group of Irish girls and women recruited or seeking to enter domestic service in America. Whether she already had a promised job or meant to seek one out on arriving in New York I can't say. Plans notwithstanding, she would marry John Flannelly at St. Peter's Roman Catholic Church in Jersey City just five years later on October 17, 1867 at the age of eighteen. John was just about to have his twenty-sixth birthday.

How and where did young Delia Hough meet Civil War veteran John Flannelly, eight years her senior? Perhaps she was a servant in the household of an affluent Jersey City family in the

Van Vorst neighborhood and crossed paths with the Flannellys at Sunday mass at St. Peter's in the mid-1860s. She may have become a friend of John's sister MaryAnn Flannelly, who was the same age as Delia, and perhaps MaryAnn introduced Delia to her big brother John when he returned from the war in 1864.

The happy news that John Flannelly was safely returned, discharged from military service, and had fallen in love with a young Irish colleen would soon be tempered by sadness and loss when John's brother Owen (age twenty-seven) passed away in November 1864. The cause or circumstance of Owen's death is not known and no official death record has been found. Owen's death, just two months after John's return home from the military, occasioned their father William's purchase of the plots at St. Peter's Catholic Cemetery in Jersey City, Owen's final resting place.

But, life goes on as it did with the 1867 marriage of your grandparents John Flannelly and Bridget (Delia) Hough. In 1868, John and Delia had their first child, a son named William, no doubt named for his grandfather William Flannelly. Their second son, Eugene (anglicized version of the name Owen), was born March 7, 1870 and was likely named for either John's deceased brother Owen or John's grandfather Owen Flannelly...or both.

The 1870-71 and 1871-72 city directories list William Flannelly, laborer, living at 124 Steuben Street. The 1870 census records William, then nearing seventy, and Mary in her mid-fifties, along with their son Edward, a carpenter, son William, age nineteen and a "teamster," and daughter MaryAnn, age twenty, a "milliner." At the time of that census-taking the family was living in Jersey City's 2nd Ward and their dwelling was number four hundred thirteen in order of visitation and their family was the nine-hundred-seventy-sixth to be recorded. Their dwelling housed five families and a total of twenty-four people including the Flannellys. One of the other tenants was a female Irish-born head of household and grocer named Margaret Carroll. The three remaining families were headed by men, one Irish-born, one English-born, and one born in New Jersey.

A closer look at the families preceding and following the Flannellys in the census-taking gives us a peek at the downtown neighborhood in 1870. The twenty-five dwellings recorded before the Flannellys' residence were home to seventy-nine families and a total of three hundred twenty-nine people, and the heads of household of those seventy-nine families were overwhelmingly Irish-born. Only nine heads of household were American-born while fifty-four were born in Ireland. The remaining heads of household were born in Scotland, England, Germany, and Canada. Similarly, the twenty-five dwelling houses surveyed after the Flannelly home housed eighty families and three hundred sixty-five people. Fifty-two of the eighty heads of household were Irish-born while only six were American-born, the remainder born in England, Germany, France, and Austria. The occupations of these Irish-born heads of household included carpenter, painter, coachman, sawyer, stationery engineer, driver, store clerk, bricklayer, blacksmith (six of those), carman, tailor, butcher, shoemaker, policeman, coach spring maker, machinist, supervisor of a locomotive shop, cooper, marble-cutter, wheelwright, railroad switchman, and merchant (six of those). The vast majority, however, were "laborers," forty-six in all. Among the few Irish households headed by women, three were listed with the occupation "charwoman." Nearly twenty-five years after the Flannellys arrived in America, they were still living downtown in an Irish-immigrant-dominated neighborhood.

The Jersey City directory for 1871-72 lists your grandfather John Flannelly, marble-cutter, living at 461 Grove Street. There was a marble-works nearby at 185 Newark Avenue and it is very possible John worked there. That marble-working business, at one time known as "Mitchell & Flannelly," had been briefly owned by Thomas Flannelly, believed to be a cousin, in the mid-1860s before changing hands and becoming Harrison & Carroll marble-works. Mitchell & Flannelly advertised as "sculptors" implying that they were marble fabricators cutting and polishing marble to order for commercial purposes. At the time Mitchell & Flannelly was in business, John's brother Owen, living at 251 South Third Street with his parents, was listed in the city directory as a marble-cutter and likely worked in his cousin's shop.

John and Delia's third son, John Jr., was born January 17, 1872. The next city directory, 1873-74, lists John Flannelly, marble polisher, living a few buildings farther down Grove Street at number 473. While still living at 473 Grove Street in March 1874, Delia gave birth to twin sons, Edward Sylvester and Frederick Aloysius Flannelly. At that time, John's directory listing showed him as a "laborer," no longer connected to marble-working it seems. Sons Eugene, John, Edward, and Frederick were all baptized at St. Michael RC Church, 252 Ninth Street, opened in 1867 and overlooking Hamilton Park. By the time of the publication of the 1874-75 city directory, John Flannelly is listed as a "laborer" and the family is still living at 473 Grove Street.

By 1876, John, still working as a "laborer," Delia and their five little boys, ages two to eight years old, had moved to 2 Ivy Place, a five-family dwelling on a short street off Grand Street near Lafayette Park. John and Delia would welcome their sixth child and first daughter in June, 1876. Annie Flannelly was baptized on July 3, 1876 at St. Patrick RC Church, Grand Street and Bramhall Avenue, built in the first half of the 1870s.

John and Delia's second (and only other) daughter was born on August 25, 1878 at 454 Grand Street. This special little girl was Mary Agnes Flannelly, your mother, gifted with the copper hair and freckles of her mother Delia. Little Mary's birth record lists her father's occupation as "car driver" and confirms that Delia had given birth to six other children, all living at the time of Mary's birth. Mary was delivered into the world by Dr. Theodore Frehlinghuysen Morris, born in New Brunswick, New Jersey in December 1831, whose office was at 301 Varick Street. Dr. Morris was a member of the native-born Protestant "genteel" class of Jersey City society. Descended from English and American Revolutionary military officers, Dr. Morris was the son of William Cullen Morris, a prominent lawyer and judge in Hudson County. The Morris family moved to Jersey City in 1849 and he began his medical studies at New York University in 1850. He was licensed in 1855 and finished his medical education at Bellevue Medical College, graduating in 1863. He was both city physician and coroner in Jersey City for some years and was a founder of the Jersey City Hospital and practiced surgery at various area hospitals.

John's parents, William and Mary Flannelly, were living at 151 Morgan Street at that time but would be living at 2 Ivy Place themselves at the time of the 1880 US census two years later along with their sons Patrick and William. William Sr. is identified on the census as being eighty years old, a laborer and disabled, having been unable to work for at least three of the prior six months. Sons Patrick and William are identified as "laborers." The Flannellys' fellow families on and around Ivy Place in 1880 were once again overwhelmingly led by Irish-born heads of household. Three-quarters of the families living in the twenty dwellings preceding and following the house occupied by the Flannellys reported Irish-born heads of household according to the census records. Seventy-seven families, a total of three hundred seventy-six individuals, lived in those forty dwellings. The Irish-born household heads indicated occupations including teamster (four of them), blacksmith, prison keeper, grocer, machinist, cooper, tailor, stableman, gardener, junkman, and washwoman. As ten years earlier, the majority of those Irish-born heads of household were listed as "laborer," thirty-one of the total fifty-seven.

What was it that these "laborers" did to earn their meager wages? They gravitated from unskilled job to job, unable to get steady employment. Those jobs were back-breaking, physically demanding, in unhealthy environments and outdoors in the elements: digging ditches, working construction sites, loading and unloading trucks or railroad cars, shoveling, lifting, and dragging as needed. In between jobs, they and their families suffered without enough food and struggled to keep a roof over their heads, begging merchants and landlords for credit to tide them over.

During the years from about 1880 through 1883, your grandparents John and Delia and their children lived at 216 Railroad Avenue, one of seven families in a dwelling housing a total of thirty-six residents at the time of the 1880 census with names including Gilligan, Morrisey, Gilmore, McGrall, McCormack, O'Neill… and Flannelly. John had started working as a porter, an occupation he would have for the rest of that decade. At the time of the 1880 US census, the two oldest children, William, age twelve, and Eugene, age ten, are attending school and the five younger children, ages two to eight, are at home with their mother. While living on Railroad Avenue, in May 1881, Delia gave birth to a sixth son, Joseph, who only lived two days. Baby Joseph was buried in the Flannelly gravesite at St. Peter's Cemetery that had been purchased by his grandfather William in 1864.

In late 1883, John and Delia Flannelly were living at 126 Newark Avenue where Delia gave birth to a seventh son, Charles Thomas, who lived for twenty-three days and died on October 4, 1883. Little Charles, like his brother Joseph, was buried in the St. Peter's family gravesite. The city directory for 1883-84 lists John J. Flannelly, porter, at 359 Montgomery Street but the 1884-85 directory lists him at 126 Newark Avenue, as does the 1885-86 directory. It is likely that some directory listings were dated or inaccurate by the time the directories, generally published every other year, came out. An eighth son, Francis Michael, was born to John and Delia in 1884. He was their last-born child and was baptized at St. Mary RC Church, opened in 1861 and located at Second and Erie Streets. John and Delia were the parents of eight surviving children, six sons and two daughters.

CHAPTER 13

Not Lost, Just Gone Before

Not all of William and Mary Flannelly's grandchildren survived childhood. Abby Flannelly, William and Mary Flannelly's oldest child, had married Michael Maloney in January 1861, the first of their children to wed. Abby Flannelly Maloney had a son Edward born in 1872. Her baby daughter, also named Abby, died in 1877 at the age of seventeen months and with the loss of that little girl, the name "Abby" was lost to future generations of girls born into our family.

In September 1875, William and Mary Flannelly's second-born son, Michael, passed away at age thirty-five and was buried in the family plot at St. Peter's Cemetery. Moreover, as the decade of the 1880s began, the future would cast a shadow over our Flannellys and the loss of family would touch and punctuate their lives each year for four consecutive years between 1881 and 1884.

As mentioned earlier, in May 1881, John and Delia Flannelly, still living at 216 Railroad Avenue, lost their two-day-old son named Joseph, who was delivered by Dr. Stephen Vreeland Morris of 212 7th Street, believed to be a relation of Dr. Theodore F. Morris, and then on October 4, 1883, lost their twenty-three-day-old son Charles Thomas.

In November 1882, your great-grandfather and family patriarch William Flannelly was stricken with pneumonia at the age of about eighty-two. After a month-long struggle, Irish immigrant William Flannelly, son of Owen and Mary Flannelly, passed away at 2 Ivy Place. His death certificate correctly reflected that he had lived in New Jersey (and Jersey City) for thirty-six years and was signed by his physician, Dr. F.W. Pettigrew, who graduated from a British medical college in 1845. William had been married to his dear wife, Mary Lang Flannelly, for fifty years, that golden anniversary having occurred eight months earlier on March 6, 1882. William Flannelly, the middle-aged tenant farmer from County Sligo, Ireland, who shepherded his wife and young children out of their homeland on a transoceanic journey predicated on the will to survive and the hope of a better future, had gone to his final, well-deserved rest.

After losing her husband, Mary Flannelly, in her early seventies, moved to 252 Railroad Avenue. The 1884 Jersey City directory has listings at that address for her sons William and Patrick, "laborers." Sadly, there is also a listing for Mary Flannelly, "washing," meaning she was taking in wash to help support herself after being widowed. It is distressing to think of her losing her partner of a half-century only to have to work so hard in the last years of her life. Not long after that directory was published, Mary developed gangrene in both legs and quickly passed away on the 28th of June 1884, exactly twenty years before your birth...to the day. I imagine her bent over a washtub scrubbing some stranger's clothes, then carrying loads of wet wash out onto a fire escape for hanging, perhaps scraping her legs on rusted grating or even falling under a heavy load of wet wash, cutting open her frail legs, leading to infected wounds ripe for gangrene...and I cringe involuntarily at the thought of such an unjust and painful end to her hard but admirable life's journey. William and Mary Flannelly, a couple for over a half-century, on two continents and across the three thousand miles of Atlantic seas, made our very existence a possibility.

William and Mary Flannelly, their son Michael, Abby Maloney's little daughter Abby, and John and Delia Flannelly's baby sons Joseph and Charles were buried at St. Peter's Cemetery in the family plot where John's brother Owen had been laid to rest in 1864.

In 1885, your grandparents John and Delia Flannelly were forty-four and thirty-six years old respectively, married eighteen years and the parents of six sons aged one to seventeen and two daughters aged seven and nine. They and John's sister Abby and brothers Patrick and Edward were then the surviving Irish-born family members. The city directories through 1886 show John working as a porter and the family living at 126 Newark Avenue. The 1887-89 directories list John J. Flannelly, porter, first at 348 First Street and then at 319 Third Street. In the nineteenth century, a "porter" meant a man who was in charge of a door or gate (such as at the entrance of a hotel) or someone who carried "burdens" such as luggage. So, we can assume that John Flannelly worked as a doorman at one or more establishments or may have worked for the local railroad loading and unloading luggage or cargo.

After the 1889 directory, there are no more listings for our John Flannelly, your grandfather. There is a reason. John Flannelly, who we know was hospitalized after the Battle of Williamsburg, Virginia, was, at least in the last years of his life, afflicted with a number of chronic illnesses and generally poor health. Today, we would call him "disabled." The federal government provided a pension program for Union veterans of the Civil War. When first created during the years of the Civil War, the legislation provided pensions for soldiers who sustained war-related disabilities and for widows and orphans of soldiers killed in action. There were multiple amendments made to the law over the next twenty-five years and those amendments had the effect of increasing the pool of eligible veterans. By 1890 Congress passed a new version of the law that made pensions available to any Union veteran who served at least ninety days, was honorably discharged, and met the disability criteria, even if the eligible disability was not the result of military service.

John Flannelly applied for a Civil War veterans pension not long after the passage of the 1890 legislation with the assistance of an attorney, R.B. Seymour. This was a pivotal point in his life and in those of his children. It was the year John would be widowed and his children made motherless. Delia Hough Flannelly, only forty years old, fell ill with pneumonia and died on March 28, 1890 at her home at 535 Monmouth Street. She left eight children, the youngest being daughters Annie and Mary, ages thirteen and eleven, and little Frank, age five. John purchased a gravesite (plot LS 67) at Holy Name Cemetery for Delia under her given name "Bridget Flannelly."

Less than a year after Delia's death, Abby Flannelly Maloney, John's older sister who had been living at 175 Brunswick Street, lost her life to chronic intestinal hepatitis at the age of fifty-five on February 8, 1891. She was buried at St. Peter's Cemetery with her parents, brothers, and her little daughter Abby. Nine months later on November 18, 1891, John's brother Patrick Flannelly died from pneumonia at St. Francis Hospital at the age of forty-eight. Patrick was not married. He too was buried with his family at St. Peter's Cemetery.

In 1892, your grandfather John Flannelly was approved for the maximum veteran's disability pension: twelve dollars per month (retroactive to 1891), his address listed as 173 Brunswick Street, next door to where his sister Abby had lived. His pension application, which includes the results of a medical examination, paints a picture of a fifty-year-old man plagued by multiple health problems. He is described as being five feet ten inches tall, weighing one hundred fifty pounds, and presenting with sallow skin, coated tongue, and the "chills." The examining doctor diagnosed John with "malarial poisoning," enlarged spleen and liver, chronic dysentery, lumbago, rheumatism, heart "failure," and impaired vision due to conjunctivitis and blepharitis.

John would only collect that pension for two years. On April 29, 1894, he died at his home at 173 Brunswick Street. His death record indicates that he succumbed to heart disease after "ailing for some months" according to Dr. Pettigrew. He was fifty-two years old. He was buried with his wife, Delia, at Holy Name Cemetery and is the only child of William and Mary Flannelly who is not interred in the family plot at St. Peter's Cemetery.

In a matter of twelve years from 1882 to 1894, death claimed all but one of the remaining Irish-born Flannellys. Only Edward remained, the youngest of the Flannelly immigrants, one year old when the family left Ireland...along with his American-born brother William and sister MaryAnn.

In February 1900, MaryAnn Flannelly David passed away at about age fifty according to the Holy Name Cemetery records. At the time, her Irish-born brother Edward was living at 213 Green Street, within walking distance of the home on Morgan's Row where he and their immigrant family first lived in the late 1840s after arriving from County Sligo, Ireland. Edward is listed on the 1900 census as a "boarder" in the Green Street house, employed as a carpenter. He passed away at age fifty-nine on May 7, 1904 at St. Francis Hospital of pneumonia. There is no evidence that he was ever married, although his death record indicated that he was married. It also incorrectly indicated he was born in the US and was fifty-six years old. Edward and MaryAnn are buried in the St. Peter's gravesite along with their parents and siblings.

With the deaths of Edward Flannelly and his sister MaryAnn, only one of William and Mary Flannelly's children remained alive: William, their last-born child, who was born in about 1851 in Jersey City some five years after the family had arrived from Ireland. William never married. He died on April 30, 1915 at the age of sixty-four. Sadly, William died of "aortic insufficiency" and arterial sclerosis at the Hudson County Almshouse in Secaucus, a facility for the impoverished or indigent. His next-of-kin was listed as Eugene Flannelly of 236 Bay Street, Jersey City and it appears that

William had lived with Eugene at some point prior to going to the Almshouse. Eugene was William's nephew, your uncle, and the son of John Flannelly, your grandfather. William is buried at St. Peter's with his parents, brothers, and sisters.

There is something of an unpleasant irony in knowing that the only American-born son of immigrants William and Mary Flannelly, who fled their homeland rather than join thousands of their countrymen seeking the awful refuge of local workhouses, would himself live out his last days at a public institution for paupers in America. Prior to the Famine, workhouses were built in Ireland to house the poor and the homeless and they were avoided at all cost by the Irish people. "Inmates" lived together in crowded, cold, and dank conditions and those able to work were put to breaking up stones. At the height of the Famine years in the late 1840s, thousands of desperate, starving, and sick Irish came to the doors of those same workhouses, which became wretched, cramped incubators of filth, deprivation, and contagious disease, where most that entered did not leave alive, buried in shallow graves nearby. On March 23, 1847, The Mayo Constitution reported:

> "In Ballinrobe, the workhouse is in the most awfully deplorable state, pestilence having attacked paupers, officers and all. In fact, this building is one horrible charnel house, the unfortunate paupers being nearly all the victims of a fearful fever, the dying and the dead, we might say, huddled together. The master has become the victim of this dread disease; the clerk, a young man whose energies were devoted to the well-being of the union, has been added to the victims; the matron, too, is dead; and the respected, and esteemed physician has fallen before the ravages of pestilence, in his constant attendance on the diseased inmates. This is the position of the Ballinrobe house, every officer swept away, while the number of deaths among the inmates is unknown;

and we forgot to add that the Roman Catholic chaplain is also dangerously ill of the same epidemic. Now the Ballinrobe board have complied with the Commissioner's orders, in admitting a houseful of paupers and in striking a new rate, which cannot be collected; while the unfortunate inmates, if they escape the awful epidemic, will survive only to be the subjects of a lingering death by starvation!"

America was and surely is the fabled "land of opportunity" but, for so many like our Flannellys, it was still a place of struggle for daily survival, of menial work, demanding physical labor for meager wages, and of only the smallest likelihood of climbing the economic ladder to a higher place in society. Our patriarch William Flannelly was a "laborer" for most of the thirty-five years he lived in Jersey City and, after his death, we know that his wife Mary, about seventy years old, resorted to "taking in wash" to help support herself. Despite over three decades in America, William and Mary still dealt with financial insecurity in their "golden" years.

And, what about their sons, those six Flannelly boys? Surprisingly, five of the six never married: Owen, Michael, Patrick, Edward, and William. The sixth, your grandfather John Flannelly, did marry (thank goodness for us who are descended of him) and, with wife Delia, had eight surviving children, two girls and six boys. William and Mary Flannelly's two surviving daughters, Abby Flannelly (Maloney) and MaryAnn Flannelly (David), also married and had children, their husbands also being "laborers."

CHAPTER 14

On the Cobblestone Streets of Jersey City

When I was a little girl there were still many original cobblestone streets in Jersey City, those cobblestones having been a mark of progress and source of civic pride at the time of their installation in the nineteenth century. For me, the announcement that we would be getting into the car to head up Tonnele Avenue provoked an immediate experience of déjà vu, and not the good kind. I had a somewhat notoriously queasy stomach that railed at bus rides and turned over in protest of *any* vehicular outings on the cobblestone streets of Jersey City. To this day, the mention of Tonnele Avenue is accompanied by a mental flashback of a 1950s car backseat (with itchy upholstery) as we jostle across the uneven cobbles and I swallow repeatedly in an effort to hold back the waves in my belly. That image is now superseded by a nostalgic appreciation for those old cobblestones that springs from a recognition that the soles of my shoes and those of my parents, grandparents, great-grandparents, great-great-grandparents, and great-great-great-grandparents all touched down on those old stones over the past century and a half.

Not only our Flannelly ancestors traversed those cobblestones. So did our Irish-born Jordan and Whalen ancestors who would join lives and give birth to their own children, including a son Patrick J. Whalen destined to marry your mother, Mamie Flannelly.

It appears that your grandmother Catherine Jordan (known as Kate) emigrated to America from her native Ireland in about 1870 when she would have been about nineteen years old. She was the daughter of Charles and Mary Ferry Jordan. On Tuesday, June 11, 1872, Kate Jordan married another Irish immigrant, Patrick Whalen, the son of Thomas and Mary Keane Whalen, age twenty-six. They were married in a civil ceremony in Jersey City. Kate and Patrick welcomed a baby girl on November 25, 1873. The baby, named Mary Whalen, was baptized at St. Mary RC Church on November 30, 1873. The 1880 US census records the family (name misspelled "Whelan") living at 400 First Street in Jersey City. Patrick's occupation is listed as "laborer."

Your grandparents Kate and Patrick Whalen lost two young children between 1874 and 1880. In 1881, their first son and your father, Patrick Joseph Whalen, was born. His birth was followed by that of a second son, Michael Joseph Whalen, in November 1882. The Whalens and the Flannellys lived in the same downtown Jersey City neighborhood. Census records and listings in city directories from the mid-1870s through 1900 find the Whalens and Kate Whalen's brothers James and Patrick Jordan and their families living at the same address or nearby each other, much of it on First Street. The Whalens lived at 388 First Street from 1874-1876 and then at 355 First Street beginning in 1877. At the taking of the 1880 census, the Whalens and both Jordan brothers' families are living at 400 First Street, a five-family dwelling. (In early records, the name is spelled as "Jordan," "Jaurdan," and "Jourdan.") James Jordan, laborer, age forty-five and born in Ireland, is listed with his wife, Helen, age twenty-eight, also born in Ireland, and their children: Charles, age six, James, age four, Helen, age two, and William, two months old. All of the children are shown as having been born in New Jersey. Patrick Jordan, laborer, age thirty-four and born in Ireland, is listed with his wife, Mary, age thirty-three and also born in Ireland, and daughter Mary J., age two, who is shown as "disabled" due to measles.

Patrick Jordan had married Mary Dallon on June 16, 1873 in Jersey City.

Based on multiple-year city directory listings beginning in 1883, your grandmother Kate Whalen was widowed near the time her son Michael was born in late 1882. In the 1883-84 and 1884-85 directories, the first of those listings appears: "Catherine Whalen, widow of Patrick," at 402 First Street, next door to where the family lived at the time of the 1880 census. By the time of the 1885-86 directory, Kate, "widow of Patrick," is still living on First Street at number 426 and her brother James Jordan has a listing at the same address in the 1886-87 directory. The 1886-87 directory lists her as Patrick's widow, living at 418 First Street. In the 1887-88 directory, widow Kate is listed at 150 York Street. Then, from 1888 to 1893, Kate and her children are living at 82 Colgate and her brother Patrick Jordan is listed at the same address. By 1897, Kate and sons Patrick and Michael are residing at 244 Wayne Street and the boys have their own directory listings, each showing their occupation as "laborer." Three years later, Kate and her two sons, neither married, are recorded at 244 Wayne Street on the 1900 US census along with nine other families, a total of twenty-six people residing in that dwelling.

At the time of that 1900 census, Kate's daughter Mary Whalen is living next door to her mother at 246 Wayne Street with her husband, Charles Wittpenn, and their newborn son, Charles. Mary and her husband had lost a child the prior year. Mary Whalen and Charles Wittpenn were married on November 10, 1898 at St. Bridget's RC Church by Father William Henry Dormin. Wedding witnesses were George McCormack and Nellie Jordan, Mary's cousin. Charles Wittpenn was a "driver" and the son of Henry and Catherine Schwartz Wittpenn, both born in Germany, and was likely a cousin of Jersey City Mayor H. Otto Wittpenn, elected in 1907 and 1909 and also the son of German immigrants.

Less than two years before your birth, your grandmother Kate Jordan Whalen, Irish immigrant and then young widow who raised three children, became ill and died of heart disease described as myocarditis on January 29, 1903. She was under the care of a young local doctor named William Leo Hetherington, who practiced nearby at 299 Varick Street and was the son of Irish immigrants himself. She passed away at her home at 244 Wayne Street. Kate's son-in-law, Charles Wittpenn, purchased a burial plot at Holy Name Cemetery and Kate was interred there a day after her death. When I discovered where she was buried after years of looking, I went to visit her and introduce myself: her great-great-granddaughter. The gravesite is marked with a tall, graceful black marble monument with curving lines, topped with a cut stone sculpted cross and the inscription "IHS," words "In Memory Of," and the names of those resting within, including "Catherine Whalen."

James Jordan's eldest son, your grandmother Whalen's nephew and the namesake of her Irish father, Charles Jordan, is found in the 1900 census, living at 30 Ferry Street in Jersey City. Charles, age twenty-five and a store bookkeeper, is married to wife, Kate, the American-born daughter of Irish immigrants. The couple has two sons, Bernard, age four, and William, age two. Charles is found in the 1910 census, a steamship company bookkeeper living at 401 Central Avenue with wife, Kate, sons Bernard, William, Charles, and Thomas, and daughter Genevieve. By 1920, Charles, age forty-five, is a bookkeeper for a "fruit house" living at 20 Bleecker Street and he and Kate have another son, John, born in 1913. At some point, Charles apparently made a conscious decision to conceal the fact that his parents, James and Helen Jordan, were Irish-born immigrants. While telling the 1900 census-taker that his parents were Irish-born, at the time of both the 1910 and 1920 censuses, Charles' parents are shown as German-born. Since both the 1910 and 1920 census records have the same information it seems a deliberate subterfuge. Perhaps in his profession as a bookkeeper for retail business firms, it was preferable not to be identified as Irish, even in early twentieth-century Jersey City.

Jersey City was a far different place in 1900 than it was when William and Mary Flannelly and their six children arrived in the winter of 1846. Multiple municipal mergers with adjacent communities such as Van Vorst Township, Hudson City, Bergen, and Greenville greatly expanded the city boundaries and total population while successive waves of European immigrants, including Irish, Germans, and then Italians, further swelled the ranks of city residents from six thousand in 1850 to two hundred thousand in 1900. Jersey City became a center for late nineteenth-century industrialization and a railroad hub as well. Large manufacturers such as M.W. Kellogg, Colgate Soaps and Perfumes, Dixon Pencil Co., Eureka Fire Hose Co., Butler Brothers, Lembeck & Betz Brewing Co., Lorillard Tobacco Factory, Great Atlantic & Pacific Tea Company, Borden Milk Co., Regina Music Box Co., and Mead Johnson (chemists) provided new types of employment in the city. Two "modern" hospitals, Christ Hospital and St. Francis Hospital, opened in about 1890, both in the downtown area where our Flannellys and Whalens lived...and died. Alexander McLean described the commerce of the city in his 1895 *History of Jersey City*:

"The city occupies a peninsula...It has a water front on each side of about six miles fronting the best harbor in the world. It is at the focus of travel and commerce. The railroad lines in Jersey City number their incoming and outgoing trains by thousands. The passengers carried annually by the eight lines of ferries leaving Jersey City have passed a billion in numbers. More ocean steamships sail from Jersey City piers than from those of any city except New York...The grain elevators on the river front are among the largest in the world. Among the manufactories in Jersey City are some of the largest of their kind; business firms whose names are household words the world over;...Smoky plumes from tall chim-

neys, and gushing steam jets, cover the business section
of the city..."

Sounds like "paradise" unless you were one of those toiling
in the smoke, steam, and noise, only to come home to a crowded tenement in the poor, largely Irish immigrant neighborhood,
where the smoke, noise, city smells, and the rumbling of the el-
evated rail tracks were waiting to greet you.

Our Irish-born ancestors who came to Jersey City in the
mid-nineteenth century spent the next half-century living on the
cobblestone streets of the oldest parts of the original Jersey City,
including in the 4th and 2nd wards, the Irish "horseshoe" district.
Looking at the census reports from 1850 to 1900, the Flannellys
and the Whalens move from apartment to apartment within the
same nearby streets: Grove, Wayne, Brunswick, Colgate, Railroad, Montgomery, Newark, and First. Were those moves due to
the growth of their families or the opportunity to live in a better
apartment or location? Or were they living from dollar to dollar,
keeping just one step ahead of a landlord they couldn't pay? I
doubt we'll ever know the answer, but the second half of the nineteenth century would see these streets sprout blocks of three-story
attached row houses framed in wood and sheathed in clapboard
siding. Some were two stories over a street-level storefront selling
provisions to the locals. Most had a front "stoop," a place to enter
the common hallway but also a place to get the air, greet and
gather with neighbors on the block. What most of them did not
have, among other things, was indoor plumbing, meaning that
chamber pots, communal outhouses, and no running water were
the norm as were the associated smells and general unsanitary
conditions.

Those streets, once an Irish immigrant enclave, would later
be the neighborhood of Italian immigrants in the early twentieth
century. Many of the row houses were long ago replaced by modern glass and steel office, residential, and commercial structures

and, on all but a precious few streets, the cobblestones are gone as well. Others have survived but are hardly recognizable, hiding under their modern skin of aluminum or vinyl siding and having lost their unique architectural flourishes. Residential gentrification in the neighborhood has resulted in the preservation of some of the nicest of these row houses, Varick Street being an example, and new luxury high-rise condominiums have joined the mix during the recent decade's real estate boom. What would William and Mary Flannelly think if they knew that a "studio" condo on Morgan Street, where they lived exactly one hundred sixty years ago, would cost them a half million dollars?

CHAPTER 15

Let All the World Say What They Will, Speak of Me as You Find

Mary (Mamie) Flannelly was born on August 25, 1878, delivered by Dr. Theo Morris at 454 Grand Street. By April, 1894, Mamie, not yet sixteen, had lost both her mother, Delia, and her father, John. She had five older brothers, one younger brother, and a sister, Annie, nearly eighteen. Mamie would be, of course, your mother.

Mamie apparently grew up fast once her parents were gone. On September 15, 1898, three weeks after her twentieth birthday, Mamie gave birth to a son, John Flannelly, at Christ Hospital on Palisade Avenue in Jersey City. The baby's birth record lists the father as John Nagle, age twenty-one and US-born, and is marked "OW," meaning an out-of-wedlock birth. When I located the birth record on microfilm at the New Jersey State Archives, one of the archivists helped me print it out. As she pulled it from the printer, she scanned it and then came a distinct "ohhhhhh" and the announcement that it was an "OW," the scarlet letter of its day. I was not surprised because you had (finally) told me the "secret" about your half-brother many, many years ago during one of my interrogations over a cup of tea but I did defensively blurt out, "I knew that" just the same.

So, who was John Nagle? I have a theory...just a theory but not improbable. I was only able to find one John Nagle of the right age in Jersey City over the period from 1880 to 1900. The 1880 census includes a Nagle family living at 161 Webster Avenue, a single-family dwelling. The family head is Samuel Nagle, age thirty, an Irish-born butcher. (In the 1870 census, Samuel is found living in Hoboken with his Irish-born mother, Ellen, and brother John and both young men list their occupation as "butcher.") In 1880 Samuel is married to Mary Scott Nagle and the couple has four children: Mamie, age eight, Michael, age six, John, age four, and Edward, age four months. Samuel is listed as a butcher. In the city directory of 1892, the family is living at 930 Summit Avenue and Samuel is a partner in a business called Kern & Nagle, which is listed in the city directory as "stables." Samuel Nagle's family was recorded in the 1895 New Jersey census and included wife, Mary, daughter, Regina, sons John, Edward, and Samuel Jr., and Ellen Nagle, his mother. The next household recorded by the census-taker was that of Michael H. Nagle, Samuel's oldest son, his wife, Dorothea Nelson Nagle, and another family, the Cables (Francis, Charlotte, and Walton).

In the 1900 federal census, Samuel Nagle, 930 Summit Avenue, is a widower and butcher living with his sons John, age twenty-three, Edward, age twenty, Samuel Jr., age thirteen, daughter Regina, age twelve, mother Ellen, age seventy-eight, and nephew Edward Nagle, age twenty-seven. This was not quite two years after Mamie Flannelly and John Nagle, then twenty-one, became the parents of an illegitimate son, John Flannelly. The 1900 census reported that John Nagle's occupation was "real estate." Samuel's older son, Michael H. Nagle, was then renting at 951 Summit Avenue with wife, Dorothea, son Samuel, age four, son Gerald, age two, and daughter Dora, age one. Like his father, Michael is a butcher.

The 1910 book *Jersey City of To-Day*, edited by Walter G. Muirhead, includes a piece on Michael H. Nagle, Samuel's ambitious and successful oldest son. Michael Nagle, photo included, is described as "engaged in the wholesale business of the handling of cattle, sheep, calves, hogs and all kinds of meat and meat products at 396 Henderson Street...the son of Samuel Nagle, who originally started in the wholesale meat business at the Central Stock Yards at the foot of Sixth Street, Jersey City." Michael had been educated in the Catholic schools of Jersey City, including St. Peter's College, and also attended the prep school of Stevens Institute of Technology in Hoboken. After graduation, Michael had joined his father's business and "his ambition prompted him later to embark into business on his own account, and he opened branch houses for the handling of cattle, sheep, veal, hogs, and other meats and meat products... One of these branch houses is in the city of Newark and is a model of its kind, doing a prosperous and extensive business."

In addition to the above businesses, the article went on to say that Michael Nagle was also the president of the recently incorporated Nagle Packing Company, his brother John F. Nagle being corporate secretary-treasurer and his brother Edward A. Nagle, vice president of the new firm. At the time the article was written in 1910, Nagle Packing was in the process of constructing a packing-house in Detroit to complement operations in Jersey City, Hoboken, Newark, and New York City. The piece closed with a glowing testament to Michael Nagle's "persistence" and "courage," his life being an "example of the fact that success is methodical and consecutive...the result of the determined application of one's abilities and powers along the rigidly defined line of labor." By 1930, Michael H. Nagle had homes in Ridgewood, New Jersey and Palm Beach, Florida, a testament to his continuing business success.

In 1910, when *Jersey City of To-Day* was published, the federal census finds John F. Nagle, the likely father of John Flannelly twelve years earlier, married to wife, Agnes, for nine years and living at 3447 Hudson Boulevard with daughters Marion, age eight, Agnes, age six, and Helen, age one. Also in the household is a twenty-year-old woman who is the children's nanny or nurse. John Nagle is the owner of their place of residence and has no sons...or did he?

Mamie Flannelly, the freckled, red-haired daughter of an Irish immigrant "porter," motherless at age twelve and fatherless as she turned sixteen, was first generation Irish-American. So was John Nagle. But that's where family similarities as to circumstances and prospects ended and that may very well be the reason Mamie found herself alone with a baby son to care for and without a husband. Did John Nagle take advantage of a young, inexperienced, love-struck girl or did he want to marry her but his family refused to allow it? And then there were her relatives: that *other* Jersey City Flannelly family from Pavonia Avenue made notorious when their son William, age twenty, shot and killed a local Jersey City girl, Mary Sexton, in their Manhattan love-nest in 1895. Every sordid detail of the couple's escapades, including their tenement rooms at a boardinghouse called "The Three Deuces" taken as Mr. and Mrs. "McCarthy" and their frequenting of "Bowery dives," was splashed across newspapers from New York to Iowa, including the pages of the venerable *New York Times*. Certainly the prosperous Nagles would have avoided association with "that kind" of family and notoriety.

I cannot say with absolute certainty that John F. Nagle was John Flannelly's birth father but I find no other viable candidate, and the fact that Mamie gave birth at Christ Hospital, near the Nagle's Summit Avenue home, may also imply a "connection" or the receipt of assistance from that family or from John Nagle himself. Or perhaps Episcopal Christ Hospital, rather than Catholic St. Francis Hospital, was simply the lesser of two difficult choices for an unwed mother.

Two years after giving birth to her son John, Mamie Flannelly appears in the 1900 census (name misspelled as "Mammie Flannery"), living with the baby at 169 Bright Street, near the corner of Monmouth Street. She, her son, and two men (Henry Dell and William Cavanaugh) were listed as "boarders" in the household of Minnie (Mary) Sigglekow (also spelled "Siegelkow"), who lived at 169 Bright Street with her sons George, age twenty, John, age fourteen, and daughter Susie, age sixteen. Minnie Sigglekow was the widow of John, a German-born barber.

Our Mamie Flannelly, boarding in the Sigglekow house with twenty-one-month-old son, John, gave her occupation as "ironer in a laundry." In most likelihood, that laundry was the Brunswick Laundry, opened in February 1898 at 298 Newark Avenue and then expanding to new quarters at 318 Newark Avenue. By 1910, Brunswick Laundry was said to be the largest starch-work laundry in Hudson County. In the late 1890s, there was a second large laundry company, Manhattan Laundry Company, located at 375-377 Wayne Street, and so it is possible she worked there if not at Brunswick Laundry. Either way, we can only wonder what it must have been like to be an unwed mother living in a boardinghouse among strangers, caring for a not yet two-year-old child, and supporting herself and her son doing ironing at a commercial laundry. But, just months later, circumstances would be changing for the better for Mamie and little John Flannelly.

On April 15, 1901, ten months after being interviewed by the census-taker, Mamie Flannelly married Patrick Joseph Whalen, son of widowed Catherine Jordan Whalen. The couple was married by a Hudson County justice of the peace and the wedding witnesses were Patrick's sister Mary and a John McLoughlin of 140 St. Paul Avenue, Jersey City. Pat Whalen gave his address as 244 Wayne Street, where he lived with his mother, his occupation as "brakeman" and gave his age as "20 years 11 months." Mamie Agnes Flannelly gave her address as 286 Wayne Street and her age as twenty-one. She was, in fact, closer to twenty-three years old. Mamie and Patrick each indicated that one of their parents, his mother and her father, was American-born, which we know was not correct. How the couple met and how long their courtship had been is not known to us but it appears that the newlyweds took up residence at Kate Jordan Whalen's home at 244 Wayne Street and Mamie brought her two-and-a-half-year-old son, John Flannelly, to the marriage.

The address Mamie gave as of her wedding day, 286 Wayne Street, was the address where her older sister Annie Flannelly was living with her Italian-born husband. Annie Flannelly had married Giovanni Bruno, known as John Brown, in 1899. Their dwelling at 286 Wayne Street was home to eight families and a total of forty-two people, including the newly married Browns and by 1901 appears to also have been the home of Mamie Flannelly and her little boy, probably through the generosity of her sister and brother-in-law.

The 1900 census, taken in June, found the Browns living at 286 Wayne and John, a truck driver, indicated that he had arrived in the United States from Italy in about 1890. A check of immigrant ship passenger records finds Giovanni Bruno, age sixteen, arriving in New York in December, 1889, in steerage class and without luggage, on the French steamer *La Normandie,* which had sailed out of the port of Havre. The ship manifest simply identified him as an "immigrant" from Italy. He has always been an intriguing figure to me because I remember you specifically telling me about him and explaining that his "real" name was Bruno but that he "went by" Brown. I wish I had asked you more about him, although over the years, in my genealogical wanderings and struggles, I have come to know him and can now tell you things about him that you did not know. For one, he was the son of Vincenzo and Vincenza Nouvello Bruno.

The Flannelly sisters, Annie Flannelly Brown and Mamie Flannelly Whalen, stayed close on Wayne Street, a cobblestone street lined with attached wood-sided row houses built in the early days of Van Vorst Township, as their young families grew with the birth of their children. In September 1900 Annie and John Brown became parents for the first time when their daughter, your cousin Rosetta

Cecilia Brown, was born on Wayne Street. In January 1902, your parents, Patrick and Mamie Whalen, had their first child together, your sister Helen. In 1903, the Browns welcomed their daughter, Anna, named for her mother. On June 28, 1904, you came into the world, the Whalens' second daughter, Catherine, at 284 Wayne Street. You were delivered by Dr. William Leo Hetherington, the same doctor who treated your grandmother Catherine Jordan Whalen at the time of her death a year earlier. In 1905, a son, Vincent, was born to your aunt and uncle Brown. The following year, on November 26, 1906, your brother William, also delivered by Dr. Hetherington, was born at 284 Wayne Street. Your cousin Margaret Brown was born the following year, 1907, but was to die in 1908 at seventeen months old. Your younger sister, Mary, named for your mother, was born at 284 Wayne Street on December 29, 1908, delivered by a Mrs. Guarino, a mid-wife. Your father, Patrick Whalen, is shown as a "driver" on your birth record and those of your brother William and sister Mary.

At the close of 1908, with the birth of your sister Mary, and the loss of little Margaret Brown, the Flannelly sisters had a total of eight surviving children, including John Flannelly, who became known as John Whalen, taking your father's name after your parents' marriage. The sisters were both at home taking care of the children, spending time with each other and with their children, nieces, and nephews. While I know that life was not easy or without privations, the strong family ties and physical proximity between the two young families must have been a positive, nurturing force. As I write these words, I am remembering you telling me about the tragic changes that would fracture the foundation of those young interwoven families just months later.

On August 2, 1909, your aunt Annie Flannelly Brown succumbed to "phthisis pulmonalis," better known as "consumption" or tuberculosis at 284 Wayne Street. She had been under the care of Dr. Hetherington and was no doubt nursed by your mother during her illness. It must have been devastating for your mother to see her sister suffer and die, leaving three young children to your mother's care. The death record shows Annie's age as twenty-nine but she, in fact, had just had her thirty-third birthday a month earlier. She was buried at Holy Name Cemetery in the gravesite she and your uncle John Brown had purchased when their baby daughter Margaret had died a year earlier.

Eight months later in April 1910 when the census-taker once again visited, the Whalens, your parents, you, your sisters Helen and Mary, and brothers William and John are renters, living at 308 Fourth Street in the Jersey City Third Ward. Also in their ex-tended household are your uncle, widower John Brown, and his children, Rosetta, Anna, and Vincent. There are no other families living at 308 Fourth Street. I imagine that your family moved from 284 Wayne trying to escape sad and still vivid memories of the loss of your aunt, it being too painful to continue living where she had suffered and died.

The census shows both your father, Patrick, and your uncle John are "truck drivers." John Brown is shown as unable to read or write English. You, your sister Helen, half-brother John, and cousins Rosetta and Anna are attending school...at St. Patrick's Catholic School. Your brother William, age three, sister Mary, age fifteen months, and cousin Vincent were at home, not yet old enough to go to school. Your mother, Mamie, must have had busy, demanding days as she had become mother to eight chil-dren after her sister's death months before and the overall "lady of the house." I have imagined her, red hair and lily-white freckled skin, getting two men off to work, five children off to school, left with three little ones at home, an apartment to keep clean, food to prepare, wash (lots of wash) to do, and a blended family to generally keep together and functioning.

As I chased the birth, death, and census records that would ultimately add clarity and detail to the story you had told me so many years ago, I read that story again and again in the rumpled pages of the notebook where I had written it down as you told it to me. So, I knew what was coming at this point of the story. Nothing could change it, then or now, but in my searching I tripped over something that would add to the story so unexpectedly as to be almost unimaginable. Some would call it "shocking" or even "scandalous." I will, for now, say I found it an amazing revelation and, for me, a gift that would bring me even closer to you and to your mother, Mamie.

As I mentioned earlier, your very definite mentioning of John Brown including the "Americanization" of his surname from "Bruno" had piqued my interest and awakened those intuitive tendencies of mine. What became of widower John Brown and your cousins Rosetta, Vincent, and Anna? I never asked you if you knew and you had never offered anything, if you did. I accessed the 1920 federal census looking for your uncle and family, and I found him. In 1920, he was still living in Jersey City, at 332 Eighth Street near Monmouth Street, and was remarried to a Catherine Tracey, who brought a son to the marriage, Alfred Tracey, age fourteen at the time of the census-taking. Your cousins Rosetta, Anna, and Vincent Brown are living with their father and stepmother and also in the household are your brother William Whalen, then fourteen, and your half-brother, John Flannelly Whalen, age twenty-one. Knowing what you had told me, I was actually relieved to see that your brothers had been under your uncle's care and roof. But there was one more person in that household, someone I couldn't account for: Joseph Brown, age seven. Since the 1920 census was taken in January, meaning that Joseph Brown was likely born in 1912, three years after Annie Flannelly Brown had died of tuberculosis, she could not be Joseph's mother. Could he be the child of John Brown and his second wife, Catherine Tracey? There was something very telling in the way the census-taker listed the John Brown household. John Brown, "head," came first, followed by Rosetta and Anna, each "daughter" and then Vincent (misspelled "Benson" probably due to John Brown's Italian accent), "son," and then

Joseph, "son." Below Joseph's name was Catherine, "wife," John Whalen, "nephew," William Whalen, "nephew," and, last, Alfred Tracey, "stepson." My intuitiveness shouted that Joseph was not Catherine's son. If he was, he would have been listed below her, not above her in the family order. If not Annie Flannelly Brown's son or Catherine Tracey Brown's son, who was Joseph Brown's mother? In my heart and in the pit of my stomach, I immediately knew the answer but how could I prove it?

By the time I got down to the New Jersey State Archives with a list of the birth, death, and marriage records I wanted to locate, I was excited and desperate to "find" Joseph Brown. I scoured roll after roll of microfilm of Jersey City births for 1911-1914 wanting to be sure I didn't miss him due to incorrect dating on the census. Since he didn't appear on the 1910 census, 1911-1914 were the key search years. I looked and looked and looked again, roll by roll of microfilm, until my eyes were crossing. No sign of Joseph's birth. After a couple hours of failure, I moved to the next item on my list, the marriage record for John Brown and Catherine Tracey. I started at 1912 and worked forward toward 1920 (the year they were found on the census as a married couple). This time all that spooling of microfilm and staring at the screen led to success. There it was: the marriage record for Catherine Fitzgerald Tracey, 404 York Street, widow of J. Tracy, born in Jersey City, the daughter of William and Mary Walsh Fitzgerald. The groom was John Bruno, 332 ½ Eighth Street, a laborer, born in Italy, son of Vincenzo and Vincenza Nouvello Bruno. The marriage took place at Holy Rosary RC Church, 344 Sixth Street in Jersey City on Saturday, November 30, 1918 at 5:00 p.m. Both bride and groom said the marriage was their second and the wedding witnesses were Giovanni Ricciardi and Jennie Muller. Father Felix DiPersia, Holy Rosary pastor who would shortly after become a monsignor, performed the marriage ceremony. Holy Rosary parish began in the 1880s as the first parish of Italian immigrants in Jersey City.

I took a minute to process that marriage information, quickly concluding that your uncle would not have waited five to six years to marry Catherine Tracey if he had fathered a son with her in 1912. Whether I should have been or not, I was happy to rule out that possibility but wondered if I would ever be able to prove my own intuitive hypothesis. Several hours had passed and my time at the Archives was winding down and then I thought of one last avenue, a definite long shot. I had accessed the 1930 federal census looking for Joseph before heading out to the Archives. He was not living with his father and stepmother in 1930. They were living alone, meaning that all four Brown children, along with your brother William and half-brother John, were out on their own as of 1930. I found Joseph, age eighteen and "single," living with his sister Rosetta, who had married a Stephen Sestanovich and had three young children of her own: Anna, age six and no doubt named for Rosetta's mother, Annie Flannelly Brown, Rita, nearly four, and Claire, nine months old, the family living at 141 Carlton Avenue, a building housing five families. Also in the household is Rosetta's brother Vincent, age twenty-five. Vincent's occupation is recorded as a clerk at a brokerage firm and little brother Joseph's as a "runner" for the brokerage.

My last hope would be to find a marriage record for Joseph. There was no real reason to believe he married but I was out of options and disinclined to give up, so no possibility was to be ignored. I pulled out the Jersey City microfilm rolls for marriages in the 1930s. If Joseph had married at the "typical" age of early-mid twenties, I might find a marriage record in the decade of the 1930s. I threw a symbolic dart and started in the middle of the decade: 1935. The gods of intuition were smiling on me. In just minutes of scanning the 1935 film, my eyes locked on a Certificate of Marriage for a Joseph John Brown. Girding myself for disappointment while slowly and deliberately moving my eyes down the page, I read the following:

Maiden name of wife: Sophie Rose Halgas
Place of Marriage: St. Peter's Church, 144 Grand Street, Jersey
    City, NJ
Date of Marriage: (Tuesday) October 1, 1935, at 11:00 a.m., by
    Rev. Dalton, SJ
Witnesses: Terence and Barbara McHugh, 309 Seventh Street,
    Jersey City, NJ
Residence of wife: 309 Seventh Street, Jersey City, NJ
Age of Bride: 26, widowed
Name of former husband: John Halgas
Birthplace: Newark, NJ
Father's Name: Joseph Niedzialkowski
Mother's maiden name: Stephania Binkowska
Residence of husband: 309 Seventh Street, Jersey City, NJ
Age of Groom: 24
Occupation: Unemployed
Birthplace: Jersey City
Father's Name: **John**

Then I involuntarily held my breath and moved my eyes down
to the next line:

Mother's maiden name: **Mary Flannelly**

Was anyone ever more pleased than I to prove that their great-
grandmother had not one but two sons out-of-wedlock? Joseph
John Brown was *our* Joseph, your brother and my granduncle.
And, he wasn't ignorant of his parentage or ashamed to acknowledge it. Victory! My mind was racing as I drove home from the
Archives, pieces of information and flashes of speculation swirling
and giving birth to new questions. It was time to knit it all together
to complete your story, warts and all.

CHAPTER **16**

And Yet to Every Bad, There is a Worse

So wrote one of my favorite nineteenth-century authors, Thomas Hardy. The death of Annie Flannelly Brown in 1909 was destined to be the starting point of one of those "things come in threes" superstitions that people swear by even today in the throes of the twenty-first century.

Sometime after the census-taker's visit in April 1910, the combined Whalen-Brown family household broke apart. Your mother, Mamie, began living with your uncle John Brown along with his children, you, your sisters Helen and Mary, and brothers John and William and, ultimately, gave birth to her sixth child, Joseph, fathered by your uncle. I have no memory or notes of you saying anything even mildly critical of your uncle, no blame, no anger, nothing negative. I cannot say the same for your descriptions of your father, Pat Whalen, who generally came off as a hard-drinking ne'er-do-well. I cannot say you hated him, though he may very well have deserved that. Apparently your sister Helen felt even more strongly against him than you did, her feelings still raw years later when expressed to her own daughter, who has since shared them with me. While we know that you and your sister were left with the scars of painful experiences with your father, the specifics and details that gave rise to those lifelong feelings remained unspoken for the most part, locked in some unreachable and unbreachable place inside each of you.

Did your mother separate from him because he was an abusive husband or father or due to his drinking? Could your mother have made a loveless marriage of convenience or opportunity, marrying Pat Whalen just to stabilize her life and that of her illegitimate son? As your mother nursed her dying sister and then consoled her widowed brother-in-law and cared for his children, could an emotional attachment have developed leading to inappropriate intimacy and discovery by your father? I am sure I will never know the answers to those questions and I suspect, having been a child between the ages of five and eight when all this was happening, even you would not be able to provide a neatly packaged explanation of just what had transpired and who was more, or less, to blame. In the end, neither of your parents nor your uncle can be labeled as strictly "saint" or "sinner," just "human."

By 1913, Mamie Flannelly Whalen and John Brown and their children were living at 226 Brunswick Street, still "in the neighborhood." By July of that year, an awful history repeated itself. Your mother, Mamie, took sick with tuberculosis ("pthisis pulmonalis"), the "consumption," the same disease that had killed her sister Annie four years earlier. She was under Dr. William Hetherington's care from July through her death on September 12, 1913 at age thirty-five. Her death certificate, in the name Mamie Whalen, identified her as a "housewife." The "informant" of her death, which had taken place at 226 Brunswick Street, was John Brown, identified as her brother-in-law and residing at the same address. There is no mention of your father on the death certificate.

I cannot possibly imagine how you felt as you saw your mother wasting away as your aunt had done, day by day, with wracking cough, sallow skin, feverish sweats, and unable or unwilling to eat. How you must have clung to her and to your uncle and how frightened you must have been. And how must it have been for your uncle to realize that he was going to lose your mother in the same cruel way he had lost her sister Annie, leaving a total of nine motherless children in his care? Death would not be denied its victory. Mamie Flannelly Whalen was buried with her sister Annie and Annie's baby daughter Margaret at Holy Name Cemetery.

I find no sign of your father having taken charge of his children following your mother's death and expected none based on what you had told me years ago. All appearances are that your uncle, John Brown, remained committed to all nine children and tried to keep the family unit together, probably with the help of his daughter Rosetta, then thirteen. Rosetta would have been old enough to help with the care of the younger children and with cooking and housekeeping, which she likely had been doing during your mother's illness. How things were organized, managed, and dealt with under such difficult circumstances I could never claim to understand or appreciate, but the motivation behind that, to provide for nine motherless children and keep them from further trauma, speaks straight to my heart and requires no explanation.

No matter how noble that objective or how hard the effort, there would be more tragedy visited upon your family, a horrific final scene that you described to me and the event that ended your childhood at age ten. On November 15, 1914, a crisp late-autumn Sunday fourteen months after your mother's death, neighborhood children of varying ages were playing outside on Brunswick Street. The last of the leaves shed by trees along the street in anticipation of the coming winter had been gathered into a low pile and then set afire. The fire had an irresistible fascination for the children on the street, the younger ones standing mouths agape when some of the older children began "jumping" the burning pile of leaves. Before long the "jumpers" were challenging the younger children to jump over the bonfire of leaves. Your sister, five-year-old Mary, too afraid to jump, was shoved forward by another child when she refused to try. Mary fell forward into the burning leaves, her clothing catching fire. She was taken to St. Francis Hospital, where she would die from her burns. Her death certificate states "schoolgirl" and "accidental burning by fire—clothing ignited from bonfire." Her last address was listed as 226 Brunswick Street. Her date of birth is incorrect. Her father's name is listed with the address "Jersey City" and his place of birth is incorrectly shown as New York. In light of those errors, it is likely that it was John Brown who provided the requested information, not your father. Your sister Mary was buried in the Holy Name gravesite owned by John Brown, laid to rest with your mother, Mamie, Aunt Annie, and your cousin Margaret Brown.

CHAPTER **17**

The White Plague

Dr. William Hetherington, who cared for both Annie Flannelly Brown and Mary Flannelly Whalen during their descent to death from tuberculosis, has been mentioned several times in the telling of your story. He was also your grandmother Catherine Jordan Whalen's doctor during her last illness and, more happily, he delivered you and your brother William.

William Leo Hetherington, good and faithful physician, was born in New York City in 1874, the son of a successful wholesale grocer named James Hetherington and his wife, Catherine Hennessey Hetherington, both born in Ireland in the 1840s and married in Manhattan in January 1871. William Hetherington graduated from the Columbia University College of Physicians and Surgeons in 1896, and despite his family's financial advantages, he opened his practice at 299 Varick Street and ministered to patients in the nearby predominantly poor downtown Irish-American neighborhood of Jersey City.

The 1900 census recorded the entire Hetherington family living at the Varick Street address and included the doctor's parents, James and Catherine Hetherington, his brothers John, James Jr., and Bartholomew, his sisters Anna and Frances, and an Irish-born servant named Mary, and, of course, William Hetherington himself. By the time of the 1910 census, the doctor's father had died (in 1904) and Dr. Hetherington is listed as the "head of household" at 299 Varick and his mother, brother James, and sister Anna are living with him. The doctor is listed as a physician in "general practice."

Dr. Hetherington, who never married, was also a surgeon associated with St. Francis Hospital in Jersey City, eventually becoming Medical Director at the hospital in about 1915. William was tall, with a medium build, gray eyes, and brown hair. I have seen him in a photo included in a jubilee publication for St. Francis Hospital. He is one of a group of St. Francis staff doctors pictured in that photo, his dark hair parted on the left and his pocket watch and chain peeking out of his vest pocket under his suit jacket.

Several years later, at the time of the great influenza epidemic in about 1918, Dr. Hetherington took ill and was eventually diagnosed with tuberculosis, the same contagious disease that had killed so many of his patients, including your aunt and your mother. Tuberculosis, we now know, is a slow-growing bacterial infection most viable when taking root in areas of the body with an abundance of blood and oxygen such the lungs. Tuberculosis is a stealthy, deadly disease capable of existing in latent form, without symptoms, in the lungs of the infected for years before becoming an active, symptomatic, and contagious form of the disease. Pulmonary tuberculosis of the lungs is spread in the exhaled breath of the infected especially through coughing, a common persistent symptom of the condition.

Although known since ancient times when it was called "consumption," tuberculosis was effectively incurable into the early twentieth century. In the third quarter of the nineteenth century, before the bacterial nature of tuberculosis was discovered, there was some belief that the disease was hereditary and unpreventable. At the end of the 1800s sanatoriums, institutions for isolating tuberculosis patients, were springing up and a regimen of rest, fresh air, and a "healthy" diet were thought to bring recovery.

Tuberculosis was primarily an urban plague, well-suited to the environment overtaking newly industrialized cities where unsanitary, crowded quarters housed the poor laboring classes, their days spent in equally crowded manufacturing settings characterized by dust, smoke, and chemical fumes. In truth, despite the conventional wisdom of the day, which saw tuberculosis as a malady of the lower class, it did not discriminate, the upper classes just as vulnerable to its contagion via contact with those infected. People caring for a patient with active tuberculosis, including doctors and nurses, were among those most likely to contract the disease. It has been estimated that in the early years of the twentieth century, as much as eighty percent of the US population was infected by the age of twenty, tuberculosis being among the most common causes of death in America.

By 1919, Dr. Hetherington, increasingly ill, had to give up the practice of medicine at the age of forty-four. Seeking the curative powers of fresh, clean air still believed to be an antidote to tuberculosis at that time, he moved to Saranac Lake, New York shortly thereafter. His sister Anna accompanied him and lived with him at 34 Military Road, a home known as one of Dr. McClellan's "cure cottages." The beautiful Saranac Lake community had become an enclave for affluent victims of tuberculosis and had been home to a sanatorium for the treatment of tuberculosis victims since the 1890s.

Dr. Ezra McClellan came to the area in the 1890s for the health of his daughter Daisietta. In about 1898, he acquired property and began to develop it, including deed restrictions ensuring that only higher-end residential dwellings could be built. Saranac Lake was also home to public hotels where invalids came to "take the air" in hopes of recovery and to the Adirondack Cottage Sanitarium, which ministered to needy patients.

Whether Dr. Hetherington thought his stay at Saranac Lake would be temporary and lead to his recovery and return to Jersey City and the practice of medicine is not known. Since he had treated so many patients struck down by tuberculosis in the prime years of their lives, he would have been keenly aware of the stages and progression of the disease and the unlikelihood of conquering it. By 1920, the Hetherington home on Varick Street was owned by a young, unmarried physician, Dr. James F. Norton.

Dr. Hetherington and his sister Anna, age forty-eight, appear on the 1920 federal census taken in Saranac Lake in January of that year as renters living at 34 Old Military Road, that lovely house still standing and occupied as of this writing. Dr. Hetherington's occupation is recorded as "medical doctor." Dr. Hetherington, a serious collector of rare books and particularly those of the Napoleonic era, would remain at Saranac Lake, dying there at age fifty-one on January 18, 1926. He was returned to Jersey City, his funeral mass taking place on the morning of January 20, 1926 at St. Bridget RC Church. His obituary, appearing in *The New York Times* on January 19, 1926, sums up the character of a good man and a deeply dedicated physician:

> "Dr. William L. Hetherington of Varick Street, Jersey City, who prior to the beginning of his illness five years ago, had a large surgical practice in Hudson County, died yesterday of tuberculosis at Saranac Lake, New York. His illness is attributed by his friends to overwork on behalf of his patients. He was a graduate of the College of Physicians and Surgeons..."

CHAPTER 18

A Tale of Two Sisters

There is no sense for me to even attempt to describe what you and your siblings were enduring in the days after your little sister was burned to death in late 1914, so soon after your mother had died. I remember you telling me, without emotion or complaint, that for two years after your mother's death and a year after your sister Mary was killed, you continued living at 226 Brunswick Street with your uncle John Brown and your cousins Rosetta, Anna, Vincent, and Joseph. Yes, you specifically mentioned little Joseph, although I will never know if you knew he was your half-brother or only knew him as one of your Brown cousins.

Considering that the seven or eight years after the deaths of your mother and sister were the years you told me the most about, you are probably asking yourself what more *I* could possibly have to tell *you*...or why I didn't end the story with your sister's death. The answer is simple: I can't stop writing your story at that point any more than I was able to stop searching and digging when I reached that chronological point in my research. The deaths of your mother and sister snuffed out the remainder of your childhood and the remnants of what was your nuclear family. What you endured and experienced after that and how you prevailed in liberating yourself and creating your own life were fused into the woman, wife, mother, grandmother, and great-grandmother you became and forever affected your personal definition of family: past, present, and future. I do now know things you never told me about those years immediately following the loss of your mother and sister, things I wish I had known when you were still here. I think it has drawn me to an even deeper understanding of you. I hope you will agree.

After the death of your mother and sister, your brothers William and John Whalen, ages eight and sixteen, stayed in the care of your uncle John Brown. A 1918 World War I draft registration record for your half-brother John Flannelly Whalen listed John Brown as his "nearest relative." John Whalen would serve in the military, some of it at Camp Zachary Taylor in Jefferson, Kentucky. In the 1920 census, William Whalen and John Whalen are found in John Brown's household along with your half-brother Joseph Brown. At the time of the taking of the 1930 census in April of that year, your brother William, age twenty-three, is a boarder in the home of John Ricciardi at 327 Eighth Street. There is little doubt that he is the same John (Giovanni) Ricciardi who was a witness at the marriage of John Brown to Catherine Tracey twelve years earlier. William would have known John Ricciardi and his family from his years of living as part of your uncle's family. So it seems that your uncle remained constant in providing oversight and a family connection for your brothers into their young adulthood.

While your two Whalen brothers were able to stay with John Brown, you and your older sister Helen would have to face the realization that you would be removed from that tenuous and fragile family unit at the ages of eleven and thirteen respectively. John Brown, more a father than an uncle for the previous four years and your last parental figure, either could not or was not allowed to keep custody of you and Helen. That meant another wave of separation and upheaval in a young life already battered by loss. Your father did not seek custody of his children, sons or daughters. You made that very clear to me and your sister did the same with her children. I can't know how you and Helen actually felt about your father shirking his parental responsibility, whether you felt the pain of abandonment or some kind of relief if he had been a hard-drinking, irresponsible father in the past. I also can't say how hard the separation from John Brown, your brothers, and cousins weighed on each of you. I do know that thirty-five years later, in 1951, when John Brown died at nearly eighty years old, he was laid to rest in Holy Name Cemetery with your Aunt Annie and your mother, Mamie, reuniting in death with the Flannelly sisters he loved in life .

By whatever reasoning process, best intentions, or path of least resistance, you and your sister were separated, each being sent to an uncle and aunt who were childless. You were sent to your father's brother, Michael Whalen, and his wife, Margaret, who were in their late twenties and were married a few years. Michael Whalen was employed as a chauffeur for E.L. Young Co. on Grand Street. Your sister was sent to your mother's brother, Edward Flannelly, and his wife, Matilda. Matilda was a Swedish immigrant who came to America in about 1902. Although she and Edward Flannelly were in their late thirties when your sister was sent to live with them, they were married only a few years as well. Edward Sylvester Flannelly was employed as a teamster driver for R.E. Dietz Co. in New York City at that time. At the time of the 1910 census, a few years earlier, the Flannellys lived in Hoboken. By 1918, they were living on Third Street in Jersey City.

Knowing that both of these couples were childless, we can assume that fact influenced the decision to send you and your sister to live with them, rather than with other aunts and uncles who had several of their own children to raise. I can't offer anything meaningful beyond the above when it comes to the time you and Helen lived with these uncles and aunts, just that those arrangements ended after about two years or so according to you and your sister Helen.

You and Helen were to be reunited when she and then you were sent to stay with your uncle and aunt, Frederick and Bella (Bridget)

Flannelly. Frederick Aloysius Flannelly was the twin brother of Edward Flannelly. He had been briefly married in about 1899 to an Irish immigrant named Mary and they had lived in New York City. Prematurely widowed not long after, he met and married Bridget Waters Pritchard, an Irish immigrant married and then widowed in New York City and with two young sons, James and Joseph, who she brought to her second marriage. The couple settled in Jersey City and lived on McAdoo Avenue at the time you were sent to live with them. Frederick was a chauffeur for the Great Atlantic & Pacific Tea Company. Fred and Bella had three surviving children of their own: Marion, James, and Edward. They lost a month-old baby son named Frederick to spina bifida in June, 1905 when they lived on Wayne Street. It was Dr. William Hetherington who signed baby Frederick's death certificate, stating that he had "attended the deceased" during his illness.

One of Bella Flannelly's grandchildren described her to me as "a hard woman." You simply called her "Bella the bitch"...always. Your sister Helen managed to coexist with your aunt because Helen had a retiring, non-confrontational personality, making her a pliable and compliant member of the household. No threat, no resistance...just survival. It was an entirely different thing with you. Oil and water all the way. I smiled when Helen's daughter, your niece Dorothy, told me how her mother described your battles with Bella. Dorothy tactfully told me that you were not the recipient of a "quiet" personality like that of your sister, quite the contrary. Your red hair, passed down from your grandmother to your mother and from your mother to you, apparently went well with your sometimes fiery personality and assertiveness. I suspect you had the effect on your aunt of a red flag waved at an irritable, territorial bull.

Although you never told me many details about how your aunt treated you except that she was a mean, nasty bitch, I eventually found out about the seminal incident that cemented your feelings against her. While you rarely ever said a bad word about anyone and did not use profanity, those rules did not apply when it came to Bella, and now I understand why. It wasn't because of the way she treated you. She wasn't the only person who wounded you when you needed love and support. It was what she did to your younger brother William.

William was the youngest of your siblings after the death of your little sister Mary. He would have been just seven years old when your mother died. The story I learned, originally told by you many years ago to the person who retold it to me, was about a day when William was visiting at Bella and Fred Flannelly's house, perhaps having come to see you and Helen. Little William either got into some mischief or just managed to somehow provoke Bella. What happened next forever drew a line in the sand. "Bella pushed William down a flight of stairs, crippling him." The words hung in my ears. *Pushed* him? *Crippled*? Now it all made sense, terrible sense.

Some weeks later, when I was speaking with your sister's daughter Dorothy, who has become my dear friend and genealogy partner, I asked her what she remembered about William, whom she had met. She said she had attended his wake for one thing. I asked her if William had any "disability." "Oh yes," she said. "He had a limp."

Perhaps your aunt didn't mean to cause William to fall down the stairs. Maybe she was angry and reckless, causing him to fall, or maybe he was trying to get away from her wrath and accidentally fell. And maybe you felt responsible for not protecting him or preventing what happened. Looking through the eyes of a child who had lost her mother and then lost her sister to a freak, avoidable accident, that fall down the stairs must have been the worst kind of déjà vu.

The die having been cast, you would leave the home of your aunt and uncle and "run away" as you told me thirty years ago. Ultimately, you would wind up in the court system, effectively an "orphan" even though your father was not dead. The well-intentioned wheels of the justice system turned, placing you as a live-in domestic servant in the home of a prosperous Jersey City Heights family by the time you were fourteen years old. Adding insult to injury, unbeknownst to you or the court, "someone" (Bella?) had misrepresented your age, making you appear at least one year older in order to get you "working papers." Whether you were thirteen or fourteen, for better or worse, the winds of change were once again blowing you on, this time leaving you on your own among strangers and completely severed from "family."

Your new "employers" were the Charles Esterbrooks of 3 Webster Avenue in Jersey City. Charles Esterbrook was born in New York in 1855, making him in his early sixties when you came to work in his home. His parents were James J. and Mary Esterbrook. James Esterbrook, born in England, emigrated from Cornwall at about age nine in the early 1830s, part of a large family believed to have been Quakers. They sailed from Liverpool on the *Gardiner* and are believed to be of the same family as Richard Esterbrook, founder of the Esterbrook Steel Pen Company. James J. Esterbrook became a naturalized US citizen in 1844 at the age of twenty-one and served in the US Army during the Mexican war in the 1840s as well, listing his occupation as "carpenter" on the enlistment record. In about 1854 he married and had a daughter named Jessie in about 1862 along with sons William (1865) and Charles (1855), all three children having been born in New York.

By the time of the 1880 census the James Esterbrook family was living at 69 Waverly Street in Jersey City and James' occupation was "carpenter." The 1880 city directory has a listing for James Esterbrook, "builder," at the Waverly Street address along with a listing for son Charles, "bookkeeper," at the same address. By 1883 the directory lists James at a new address, 70 Reservoir Avenue. Listings for him at that address continue through 1888, each showing him as a carpenter or builder. During the same period, son Charles is listed at the same address, first as a bookkeeper, but then as a "deputy collector." In 1889, the city directory had listings for James Esterbrook and for both of his sons, Charles and William, who was a "clerk," all three living at 3 Webster Avenue.

City directory listings in the early to mid-1890s include a large, boldface type listing for **Charles Esterbrook, Clerk-Board of Fire Commissioners** at 3 Webster Avenue. The 1900 federal census records Charles, wife Mary Ellen, and three children living at 3 Webster Avenue. Fifteen years later, when you lived and worked in their home, you would cross paths with at least two of those children, son Charles Jr. born in about 1899 and daughter Jessie born in about 1896.

Alexander McLean's *History of Jersey City*, published in 1895, in a chapter titled "Biographical Sketches of the Men who are Prominent in the City's Affairs Today" included a piece on Charles Esterbrook saying that he attended school until the age of fifteen, then went to work for a shipping and commission house in New York City until 1886 when he took a position as deputy collector of revenue in Jersey City and then, in 1889, became clerk to the Board of Fire Commissioners. Charles Esterbrook was (obviously) active in local politics, having been secretary to the Hudson County Democratic Committee in 1885 and then served as chairman of that organization. He was also a member of the Ancient Order of Foresters and the Berkeley Club.

You never told me much about your time working and living in the Esterbrook house over the several years you stayed there except to say that you were paid twelve dollars a month. The house at 3 Webster is still there, although the Esterbrook family no longer had ownership of it by 1930 when it was owned by a doctor, Thomas Brennick. The Esterbrook "children," Jessie and Charles, by then in their early thirties, are found on the 1930 census living in what must have been a large apartment building at 145-147 Harrison Avenue. Charles is unmarried and his sister Jessamine indicated she was divorced. They are paying eighty dollars per month rent and, judging by that and the professional occupations of the other tenants, the building must have been upscale. Jessie gave her occupation as "school teacher" and Charles as "prohibition investigator." Like father, like son...in the mix of local government.

In my quest to document your story, I sought out the current owner of the house at 3 Webster Avenue. The house has only been owned by three families in its 120 years of existence: the Esterbrooks, Dr. Brennick, and the Restivos. Dr. Carl Restivo's grandmother purchased the house from Dr. Brennick in helping her son, also a doctor, in the early years of his practice and marriage in the 1940s. The Restivo family has owned the house ever since and it served as family home and medical office for the first Dr. Restivo and now as medical offices for his son Dr. Carl Restivo, who graciously invited me to visit 3 Webster. Although the house is much changed from what you would have known ninety years ago due to the conversion to medical offices and general modernization, I did my best to channel you as Dr. Restivo showed me through the house, including the basement where I am sure you did wash and other chores. I saw the dumbwaiter you probably used to move laundry and provisions to and from the basement and upper floors. As I passed through what I knew was a wide original hall doorway made of old oak patinated with decades of old varnish resembling the color of maple syrup, I ran my hands across the wood of the door and doorframe, hoping to fuse my palms with remnants of yours left there nearly a century before.

CHAPTER **19**

Wife and Mother...and Daughter

Your time at the Esterbrook home would end on Tuesday, January 18, 1921 when you married Pop, a pipefitter and twenty-year-old son of German immigrants living on Terhune Avenue. At the time you made this life-changing decision, the first of your young life made by *you*, you believed yourself to be seventeen and a half years old based on those falsified work papers. You were, in reality, just sixteen and a half. Still respecting your Catholic upbringing you convinced Pop, who was raised in a large churchgoing Lutheran family, to marry in the rectory of St. Joseph's Catholic Church at 511 Pavonia Avenue in Jersey City. The ceremony was performed by Father James Owens at 3:00 p.m., witnesses being Matthew Boylan and Catherine Higgins.

As you were exerting your own independence in pursuit of personal freedom, your ancestral countrymen were doing the same in our Irish homeland. Ireland's eight-hundred-year quest to be free of British domination and oppression, reignited by the Easter Rising in Dublin and kept aflame in guerilla-warfare skirmishes, would finally succeed in the rebirth of an independent Irish state in the early 1920s and the return of the right of self-determination to its people.

Your own first freely made life decision gave birth to a wonderful marriage of over fifty years, six children, thirteen grandchildren, including me, and a dozen great-grandchildren. My mother, Arlene, your only daughter, has a simple but powerful way of describing the mother you were: "My mother worked so hard. She 'did' for *everyone* and she did *everything* for us."

The 1930 census recorded your family living at 81 ½ Terhune Avenue, where you were paying a rent of thirty dollars a month, quite a difference from the eighty dollars rent the Esterbrooks were paying at the same time for their apartment. Pop listed his occupation as "gas maker" at a gas factory. By the early 1930s, you and Pop had five sons along with my mother. And that's when you became a "daughter" again.

Your "father," the long-absent Patrick Joseph Whalen, struggling with alcohol abuse and declining health, came knocking, looking for help. Whether you wanted to or not, you didn't slam the door in his face as so many people would have done. He had long since ceased to be a parent to you and represented a vivid reminder of painful memories of a life and a family that you had purposefully left behind when you joined Pop's welcoming family and bonded with them, making them your family as well.

Where had old Pat Whalen been for the last near-twenty years? He had been knocking around, drinking his way through years in the US Army, managing to marry again and become a widower for the second time a decade earlier. I tracked down his military record, an abstract only, due to a catastrophic fire in 1973 that consumed the majority of government military records, some eighteen million files having been lost. Much of his surviving service record had to do with his serial visits to Army doctors complaining of an array of maladies and symptoms.

Pat enlisted in the Army for the first time on November 21, 1917 and served as a private with the 139th Aeronautical Squadron, his service ending on April 17, 1919. Being thirty-six years old and over the age limit for enlistment, he lied on his application, giving a birth date of 1885, representing himself as thirty-two instead. You told me how he showed up at the Esterbrook home unexpectedly one day around this time. He just rang the doorbell, in uniform, introduced himself, and asked for you, his "daughter." I grit my teeth when I remember that you told me Mrs. Esterbrook invited him in and asked him to stay for a bite to eat, which you wound up serving to him. That man was just shameless!

Just a week after being discharged in April 1919, he re-enlisted and served for another year as a private in a "machine gun company." He listed his emergency contact as his sister Mary Whalen, address: 199 Wayne Street. At the time he did this, his sister was married to her second husband and her name was Mary McNally. Perhaps he didn't realize that. Somewhere in that time period, he met and married Alice O'Connor, born in West Point, New York in 1881, the daughter of John and Mary O'Connor, both born in Ireland. At the time of the 1920 federal census, which was taken in January of that year, Alice O'Connor Whalen, thirty-eight, married and a "labeler" at a can factory, is living alone (Pat being in the Army) at 274 Monmouth Street, near Varick. Pat was discharged three months later in April 1920, and presumably went home to Alice. Ironically, Alice Whalen would be struck down with the same disease that took Pat's first wife, your mother: tuberculosis. Alice was hospitalized on November 2, 1922 at the Hudson County Tuberculosis Hospital located in Secaucus and died there on December 16, 1922 at the age of forty-one. Her death certificate listed her husband's name as Patrick Whalen and her home address as 167 Bright Street in Jersey City, that house being next door to the house where your unwed mother and baby son were boarders in 1900. In another case of history repeating itself, Alice Whalen's burial was not in a gravesite purchased by her husband. She was buried in the plot at Holy Name Cemetery owned by Pat's sister Mary Whalen Wittpenn McNally, with Pat's mother (your grandmother), Catherine Jordan Whalen.

About a year after Alice's death on December 10, 1923, Pat Whalen once again re-enlisted in the Army and remained in the military until January 5, 1927. He was a PFC in the medical department at Fort Totten, New York. He "re-upped" one last time at the expiration of that term of service, giving his emergency contact as you, Catherine Whalen, 106 Greenville Avenue, and was finally discharged as a corporal in the Station Hospital Medical Corp on February 8, 1928. At the time of discharge, he gave his future address as "Lakewood, General Delivery." The Lakewood connection might have been a reference to the poultry farm there owned by Pop's mother, where perhaps he thought he could hang up his hat among the chickens.

Between 1925 and 1927, Pat both served in a medical unit of the Army and was a regular patient as well. In August 1925, his records indicate hospitalization on the US Army Transport ship *St. Mihiel* for pulmonary observation, leading to treatment for five months for active tuberculosis and pleurisy at Station Hospital, Fort Totten. A month later, in March 1926, he was hospitalized for acute influenza at Fort Totten. In April of the same year, he was treated for acute arthritis of the shoulder and elbow joints. Then, in July 1926 he was hospitalized for both acute arthritis and chronic tonsillitis, resulting in a tonsillectomy.

In January 1927, in preparation for discharge, a medical exam diagnosed him with inactive chronic pulmonary tuberculosis with lesions in his lungs in the left upper lobe and right upper and middle lobes. The lesions presented as "healed." After his immediate re-enlistment the same month, the results of Pat's colorful past and lifestyle caught up with him and in February 1927 were documented for posterity by the Army doctor at Station Hospital, Fort Totten as "chronic alcoholism." He would be readmitted to Station Hospital the following month, where he received a sinusotomy for "acute left maxillary sinusitis." The last medical entry is dated October 1-6, 1927, when he was hospitalized at Fort Totten for acute pharyngitis, a viral infection of the upper respiratory tract, characterized by low fever and swollen lymph nodes. The majority of Pat's maladies, excluding his alcoholism of course, were ultimately designated as having occurred "in the line of duty," qualifying him to receive a military pension.

By the census of 1930, your father, Pat Whalen, "unemployed," is one of three adult male boarders in the downtown apartment of a forty-six-year-old widow named Ellen Lenney in a dwelling housing a total of three families at 133 Railroad Avenue in Jersey City, the same street where your Flannelly grandparents had lived a half-century earlier. The journey had come full circle "in the neighborhood." Presumably Pat was living off his Army pension.

His health continuing to fail as his drinking kept up, he turned to you for help. My mother recalls him sleeping on a cot in your kitchen and remembers him relentlessly following you room to room begging for money for liquor when he had run through his pension check. "Kate, give me a quarter, Kate give me a quarter, Kate give me a quarter," over and over and over. She also remembers stories of her older brothers locking him in the basement to get him out of everyone's hair.

Patrick Joseph Whalen, son of Irish immigrants, raised by a persevering widowed mother, husband to a young woman with an illegitimate son, father of four, who he abandoned to the care of others, and chronic alcoholic, died on March 11, 1935 of acute pancreatitis. He had been hospitalized at the Jersey City Medical Center for ten days prior to his death and had pancreatic surgery on March 3, 1935 in a last attempt to save his life. His death certificate lists you as his next of kin and then living at 370 Pearsall Avenue, Jersey City. In the end, Pat was to spend his afterlife in much the same fashion as he had lived on earth: alone, buried by himself in a soldier's plot at Holy Name Cemetery.

CHAPTER **20**

Marking Time

Just recently, your sister's daughter Dorothy and I went "cemetery-hopping." The discovery of multiple ancestral family graves at St. Peter's and Holy Name meant the opportunity to visit the relatives and pay our respects. But first, there were some "housekeeping" issues, some situations to put right.

The gravesite where your grandparents John and Delia Hough Flannelly were laid to rest at Holy Name has a nice headstone, installed in the mid-twentieth century. Inscribed on the stone were the names John Flannelly, Frederick Flannelly, and Bridget Flannelly. Yes, it is also the final resting place of your uncle Fred Flannelly and his wife Bella…the bitch. But somehow, the person who had the monument made was apparently unaware that the first occupant of that grave was Delia Flannelly and so her name was not inscribed on the headstone. In recent months, that oversight was corrected and Delia, "lost" for over a century, is now found and remembered.

I am sure you will remember that day over thirty years ago when you, my mother, and I went to Holy Name Cemetery in search of your mother's grave and found it without a grave-marker of any kind. It was a moment of mixed emotions, happy to have found her, sad to see the grave without a headstone. Just two weeks ago, a tasteful gray granite marker was set in place on your mother's grave, a gift from my mother, your niece Dorothy, and me. It remembers all those laid to rest in that gravesite: Anna Flannelly Brown, your aunt; Margaret Brown, your baby cousin; Mamie Flannelly Whalen, your mother; Mary Whalen, your little sister; and, the "man of the family," your uncle, John Brown. One hundred years after John Brown purchased that grave, it was finally marked in remembrance of your family and topped off with a bouquet of autumn flowers.

We also visited your grandmother Catherine Jordan Whalen's grave that day, shared with her daughter Mary Whalen Wittpenn McNally and with your father's second wife, Alice O'Connor Whalen. And, we stopped by the soldier's section to check on your father. His chalky white headstone shows the effect of the passing of the last seventy-five years but the inscription is still legible:

Patrick J. Whalen
New Jersey
Pvt. 139th Aero Sq
March 11, 1935

We also made our first, long-awaited visit to St. Peter's Cemetery on Tonnele Avenue that day. We had to arrange for someone from Holy Name to meet us there and open the locked cemetery gates. We were guided to the Flannelly gravesite, the plots purchased by your great-grandfather (my great-great-great-grandfather) in 1864 at the death of his twenty-seven-year-old son Owen Flannelly, then a recent Civil War veteran. Over the next century, a total of seventeen members of our Flannelly family, spanning four generations, were laid to rest there. We were standing where our ancestors once stood, we were remembering on the very spot where they mourned. It is marked with a tasteful granite headstone inscribed "FLANNELLY" on which we placed another of those autumn bouquets.

We made one other cemetery stop that day, at Bayview Cemetery, the expansive non-sectarian cemetery straddling both sides of Garfield Avenue and dating to the 1840s. The section of the cemetery that spilled across Garfield Avenue slopes downward to a view of New York City in the distance and is where you and Pop were laid to rest. Your grave is marked with a small, flat gray granite slab, the only form of marker allowed by cemetery regulations. I crouched down in front of the marker, which has sunk into the soft ground over the years, and pulled out clumps of grass and weeds encroaching on the marker and forming an obstructive fringe around its edges. I patted the gravestone as if it were an extension of you as I quietly said a few words, telling you about the day's adventures. The cemetery rules, prominently posted on a billboard nearby, say "no flowers." I smiled and, inspired by you, pushed the metal spike of the plastic flower holder into the ground and filled it with the last of the autumn bouquets.

Descendants of Owen Flannelly

1-<u>Owen Flannelly</u> b. Cir 1775, Ireland, d. Ireland
+<u>Mary</u> b. Cir 1775, Ireland, m. Unknown, Ireland, d. Ireland
2-<u>William Flannelly</u> b. Cir 1800, Ireland, d. 1882, Jersey City NJ
+<u>Mary Lang</u> b. Cir 1812, Ireland, m. 1832, Skreen, County Sligo, Ireland, d. 1884, Jersey City NJ

3-Eleanora Flannelly b. 1834, Sligo, Ireland, d. Unknown, Sligo, Ireland
3-Abby Flannelly (Maloney) b. 1835, Sligo, Ireland, d. Feb 1891, Jersey City NJ
3-Owen Flannelly b. 1837, Sligo, Ireland, d. Nov 1864, Jersey City NJ
3-Michael Flannelly b. 1839, Sligo, Ireland, d. Sep 1875, Jersey City NJ
3-Patrick Flannelly b. 1843, Sligo, Ireland, d. Nov 1891, Jersey City NJ
3-Edward Flannelly b. 1845, Sligo, Ireland, d. May 1904, Jersey City NJ

3-MaryAnn Flannelly (David) b. 1849/50, Jersey City NJ, d. Feb 1900, Jersey City NJ

3-William Flannelly b. 1851/52, Jersey City NJ, d. May 1915, Jersey City NJ

3-<u>John Flannelly</u> b. Oct 1841, Skreen, County Sligo, Ireland, d. 29 Apr 1894, Jersey City NJ

+<u>Delia (Bridget) Hough</u> b. 1848/49, Ireland, m. 17 Oct 1867, St. Peter's RC Church, Jersey City NJ, d. 28 Mar 1890

4-William Flannelly b. 1868, Jersey City NJ

4-Eugene Flannelly b. 7 Mar 1870, Jersey City NJ

4-John Flannelly b. 17 Jan 1872, Jersey City NJ

4-Edward Flannelly b. 24 Mar 1874, 473 Grove St., Jersey City NJ

4-Frederick Flannelly b. 24 Mar 1874, 473 Grove St., Jersey City NJ

4-Annie Flannelly (Brown) b. Jun 1876, Jersey City NJ, d. 1909, Jersey City NJ

4-Joseph Flannelly b. May 1881, Jersey City NJ, d. May 1881, Jersey City NJ

4-Charles Thomas Flannelly b. Sept 1883, Jersey City NJ, d. 4 Oct 1883, Jersey City NJ

4-Francis Michael Flannelly b. 5 Sep 1884, Jersey City NJ

4-<u>Mary (Mamie) Flannelly</u> b. 25 Aug 1878, 454 Grand Street, Jersey City NJ, d. 12 Sep 1913, Jersey City NJ

+<u>Patrick Whalen</u> b. 1880, Jersey City NJ, m. 15 Apr 1901, Jersey City NJ, d. 11 Mar 1935, Jersey City NJ

5-John Flannelly Whalen b. Sep 1898, Jersey City NJ (Son of John Nagle)

5-Helen Whalen b. 1902, Jersey City NJ

5-**Catherine (Kate) Whalen** b. 28 Jun 1904, Jersey City NJ, d. Jan 1988, NJ

5-William Whalen b. 1906, Jersey City NJ

5-Mary Whalen b. 1908, Jersey City NJ, d. Nov 1914, Jersey City NJ

+**John Brown** b. 1872, Italy, d. 1951, NJ

– Joseph John Brown, b. 1912, Jersey City NJ

Bibliography

General Historic Records and Documents Sources:
United States Census Records: 1850-1930. Ancestry.com. 2008-2009. <http://www.ancestry.com>

New Jersey State Census: 1895. Ancestry.com. 2008-2009. <http://www.ancestry.com>

United States Military Draft Registration Records: World War I and World War II. Ancestry.com. 2008-2009. <http://www.ancestry.com>

Jersey City, New Jersey Directories: 1880-1900. Ancestry.com. 2008-2009. <http://www.ancestry.com>

Jersey City, New Jersey Directories: 1849-1885. New Jersey Room, Jersey City Free Public Library. 2009.

New Jersey Birth, Death and Marriage Records: 1848-1935. New Jersey State Archives. 2009.

Jersey City History Sources:
Jersey City Past And Present. New Jersey City University. 2009. <http://www.njcu.edu/programs/jchistory/About.htm>

McLean, Alexander. *History of Jersey City, New Jersey.* Jersey City: F.T. Smiley & Co., Jersey City Printing Co., 1895.

Muirhead, Walter G. *Jersey City of Today.* Jersey City: 1910.

Petrick, Barbara Burns. *Church and School in the Immigrant City 1830-1930*. Dissertation Abstract: 1995.

Shalhoub, Patrick J. *Images of America: Jersey City*. Dover, NH: Arcadia Publishing, 1995.

Shaw, Douglas V. *The Making of an Immigrant City*. New York: Arno Press, 1976.

Ireland/Irish History Sources (General History, Famine, Emigration):

1824 Tithe Applotment – Ireland –Doonflin Upper, Skreen, County Sligo. Flannery Clan. 2009. <http://www.flanneryclan.ie>

A Timeline of Schooling in Sligo. Rootsweb. 2009. <http://www.rootsweb.ancestry.com/~irlsli/school6.html>

Asenath Nicholson. University College of Cork. 2009. <http://multitext.ucc.ie/d/Asenath_Nicholson>

Bennett, William. *Six Weeks in Ireland*. London: Charles Gilpin, 1847.

Carleton, William. *The Black Prophet*. London: Charles H. Clarke, circa 1850 (no date given).

Day, Angelic and Patrick McWilliams. *Ordnance Survey Memoirs of Ireland Volume 40, Counties of South Ulster 1834-38*. Belfast: The Institute of Irish Studies, 1998.

Dolan, Jim. *The Irish Are Coming: Sligo to Scranton 1850-1900*. Sayre, PA: Clare Printing, 2008.

Doonflin Upper – Real Property Records 1858-2002. Dublin: Valuation Office

Flannelly, Patrick. *The Great Famine 1845-1852: Attymass Parish*. 1946. <http://www.attymass.ie/historical_documents/famine/famine_flanelly.pdf>

Gallagher, Thomas. *Paddy's Lament*. New York: Harcourt Brace Jovanvich, 1982.

Hall, Mr. & Mrs. S.C. *Ireland, Its Character and Scenery*. New York: A. W. Lovering, 1841.

Hollett, David. *Passage to the New World*. Gwent, Great Britain: P.M. Heaton Publishing, 1995.

Ireland. Excerpt from English schoolbook, 1792 (author & publisher unknown).

Irish Famine. Vassar College. 2009. <http://adminstaff.vassar.edu/sttaylor/FAMINE/ILN/Index.html>

Irish Potato Famine. The History Place. 2009. <http://www.historyplace.com>

Laxton, Edward. *The Famine Ships*. New York: Henry Holt and Company, Inc., 1996.

Lissadell House, Coffin Ships, The Pomano & Sir Robert Gore Booth. Sligo Heritage. 2009. <http://www.sligoheritage.com/archpomano.htm>

Mangan, James J. *Gerard Keegan's Famine Diary*. Dublin: Wolfhound Press, 1991.

McTernan, John C. *Memory Harbour*. Sligo, Ireland: Avena Publications, 1992.

McTernan, John C. *Olde Sligoe*. Sligo, Ireland: Avena Publications, 1995.

Melville, Herman. *Redburn*. New York: Library of America, 1983.

Nicholson, Asenath and Maureen Murphy. *Annals of the Famine in Ireland*. Dublin: Lilliput Press, 1998.

Nicholson, Asenath. *Ireland's Welcome to the Stranger*. New York: Baker and Scribner, 1847.

Norton, Desmond. *Landlords, Tenants, Famine*. Dublin: University College Dublin Press, 2006.

O'Connor, Joseph. *Star of the Sea*. Orlando: Harcourt, Inc., 2002.

Preteseille, Landry. *Master's Thesis*. Centre d'Etudes Irlandaises de L'Universite Rennes 2, Haute Bretagne. 2009. <http://www.dennyhatch.com/jackcorbett/doc/IrishEmigration.pdf >

Quinn, Peter. *The Tragedy of Bridget Such-A-One*. <American Heritage.com/immigration/articles/magazine/ah/1997/8/1997_8_36.shtml>

Scally, Robert J. *The End of Hidden Ireland*. New York: Oxford University Press, 1995.

Sligo County Library – Local Studies Department. Sligo, Ireland, 2008.

Somerville, Alexander and K.D.M. Snell. *Letters from Ireland During the Famine of 1847*. Dublin: Irish Academic Press, 1994.

Swords, Liam. *In Their Own Words: The Famine in North Connacht 1845-1849*. Dublin: The Columba Press, 1999.

Thebaud, Rev. Aug. J. SJ. *The Irish Race in the Past and in the Present*. New York: Peter F. Collier, 1879.

de Tocqueville, Alexis and Emmet Larkin. *Journey in Ireland*. Washington D.C.: The Catholic University of America Press, 1990.

Tuke, James Hack. *A Visit to Connaught*. London: Charles Gilpin, 1848.

Woodham-Smith, Cecil. *The Great Hunger*. New York: Old Town Books, 1962.

Workhouse: Sligo, County Sligo. The Workhouse Website. 2009. <http://www.workhouses.org.uk>

Tuberculosis Information Sources:

Dubos, Rene and Jean Dubos. *The White Plague*. New Brunswick, New Jersey: Rutgers University Press, 1996.

History of Saranac Lake. Historic Saranac Lake (wiki). 2009. <http://hsl.wikispot.org/A_History_of_Saranac_Lake>

Ott, Katherine. *Fevered Lives*. Cambridge, MA: Harvard University Press, 1996.

Ryan, Frank, MD. *The Forgotten Plague*. Boston: Little, Brown and Company, 1993.

Civil War Information Sources:

American Civil War Regiments: Regimental History – New Jersey 6th Infantry. Ancestry.com. 2008-2009. <http://www.ancestry.com>

American Civil War: The Soldier's Life. Thomas Legion. 2009. <http://thomaslegion.net/soldier.html>

American Civil War: 1865. 2009. <http://www.spartacus.school-net.co.uk/USAcivilwar6.htm>

Battle of Williamsburg. Virginia War Museum. 2009. <http://www.peninsulacampaign.org>

Bellard, Alfred and David Herbert Donald. *Gone for a Soldier*. Boston: Little, Brown & Company, 1975.

Desertion in the Civil War Armies. Thomas Legion. 2009. <http://thomaslegion.net/americancivilwardesertionsunionandconfederate.html>

Dysentery and Diarrhea – Civil War. 2009. <http://www.wtv-zone.com/civilwar/dysentery.html>

Foster, John Y. *New Jersey and the Rebellion*. Newark: Martin R. Dennis & Co., 1868.

Hastings, Earl C. and David S. Hastings. *A Pitiless Rain*. Shippensburg, PA: White Mane Publishing Co., 1997.

Hudson, Carson O. Jr. *Civil War Williamsburg*. Williamsburg, VA: Colonial Williamsburg Foundation, 1997.

Stryker, William. *Record: Officers and Men of New Jersey – Civil War 1861-1865 Volumes I and II*. New Jersey, 1876.

The Civil War Letters of the Fox Brothers. Ohio State University. 2009. <http://ehistory.osu.edu/osu/sources/letters/fox/index.cfm>

Union Medical Civil War Facts. 2009. <http://www.nycivilwar.com/facts/usa/usa-medical.htm>

Book Cover Images:

Front cover photo: Courtesy of Jersey City Free Public Library, New Jersey Room

Maps: From the author's personal collection

Additional Suggested Reading:

Cahill, Thomas. *How the Irish Saved Civilization*. New York: Doubleday, 1996.

Sykes, Bryan. *The Seven Daughters of Eve*. New York: W. W. Norton & Company, 2002.

Sykes, Bryan. *Saxons, Vikings and Celts*. New York: W. W. Norton & Company, 2007.

LaVergne, TN USA
08 March 2010
175215LV00001B/1/P